Reinventing Schools

It's Time to Break the Mold

Charles M. Reigeluth and Jennifer R. Karnopp

ROWMAN & LITTLEFIELD EDUCATION

A division of
ROWMAN & LITTLEFIELD PUBLISHERS, INC.
Lanham • New York • Toronto • Plymouth, UK

Published by Rowman & Littlefield Education
A division of Rowman & Littlefield Publishers, Inc.
A wholly owned subsidary of The Rowman & Littlefield Publishing Group, Inc.
4501 Forbes Boulevard, Suite 200, Lanham, Maryland 20706
www.rowman.com

10 Thornbury Road, Plymouth PL6 7PP, United Kingdom

British Library Cataloguing in Publication Information Available

Library of Congress Cataloging-in-Publication Data

Reigeluth, Charles M.
  Reinventing schools : it's time to break the mold / Charles M. Reigeluth and Jennifer R. Karnopp.
     pages cm
  ISBN 978-1-4758-0239-9 (cloth : alk. paper) — ISBN 978-1-4758-0240-5 (pbk. : alk. paper) — ISBN 978-1-4758-0241-2 (electronic) 1. School improvement programs—United States. 2. Educational change—United States. I. Karnopp, Jennifer. II. Title.
  LB2822.82.R43 2013
  371.2'07—dc23   2013016922

∞™ The paper used in this publication meets the minimum requirements of American National Standard for Information Sciences—Permanence of Paper for Printed Library Materials, ANSI/NISO Z39.48-1992.

Printed in the United States of America

We dedicate this book to Morgan, Eliza, Jillian, Dane, and all other children who so desperately need an educational system that is designed to meet their needs.

Contents

Figures and Tables

Preface

In the United States, elementary and secondary students do not measure up well when standing toe to toe with their international peers. But this isn't breaking news. For decades, national oversight groups and independent experts have been issuing data and reports like *Nation at Risk* (published in 1983 by the National Commission on Excellence in Education) and the *U.S. Education Reform and National Security* report (published by the Council on Foreign Relations in 2012) that strongly decry the performance of U.S. schools.

The U.S. Department of Education (along with all fifty of the U.S. state departments of education and many private foundations) have poured billions of dollars into elementary and secondary educational reforms since the Russians launched Sputnik in the 1960s, yet U.S. public schools are still not meeting the educational needs of many of their students. Clearly, the current approaches to educational reform are failing.

This book explores why the current approaches are failing and what kinds of approaches are needed. Specifically, we look at the existing education structure in the United States and how it needs to change to meet the current and near-future learning needs of students. We describe two aspects of education reform: what education systems should be like from preschool through high school, and how to help current systems transform themselves accordingly.

Chapter 1 explores the fundamental changes in society as the Industrial Age evolved to the information age and describes how the educational needs of students and communities have changed to accommodate this shift. This chapter points out that *what is taught* (the content) and *how it is taught* (the instructional methods) need to change. Yet perhaps more importantly, we provide evidence that the *fundamental structure* of the U.S. education system has become obsolete—if not actually counterproductive to meeting the new educational needs.

This chapter provides evidence that the current education system is structured to leave children behind and describes an alternative structure—that maximizes learning while lowering educational costs—to meet the new education needs of the information age.

Chapter 2 uses an analysis of key differences in society between the Industrial Age and the Information Age to present a vision of an educational system that can meet the educational and developmental needs of students and their communities in today's world—in a way that's more cost-effective than the current system. This chapter describes six core ideas to stimulate thinking about what is possible for education:

1. an attainment-based system
2. learner-centered instruction
3. expanded curriculum
4. roles for students, teachers, and technology that support self-directed learning
5. a nurturing school culture
6. decentralized organizational structures

Furthermore, features of current education systems that are counterproductive to student learning are identified. Finally, this chapter addresses the cost-effectiveness of the new system.

Chapter 3 highlights three examples out of hundreds of school systems that have already adopted the new kind of system that we envision in chapter 2. These examples represent change at various levels of education—a single school, a school district, and an international school model—and describe how the three organizations use the six core ideas that are introduced in chapter 2 along with evidence of each organization's effectiveness. An appendix lists many similar school systems.

Chapter 4 outlines how to transform existing schools and design new schools to achieve the Information Age education system on a small scale (individual schools), medium scale (school districts), and large scale (state systems). The chapter identifies principles of change that can help guide any transformation process, and it explores "open questions" that can influence the success of a transformation effort.

Chapter 5 proposes initiatives that the federal government can undertake to accelerate the transformation of school systems: supporting developing a new kind of technological tool, piloting best practices, building states' capacity to facilitate change, and advancing knowledge about the paradigm change process. A phased approach is recommended for each of these four initiatives.

There is a fairly detailed summary of key ideas at the end of each chapter. More information is available at www.reinventingschools.net, and we welcome your input on our blog or Facebook page through that website.

Acknowledgments

We are especially grateful to Jenny Brown for her excellent editing of our work. We are thankful to Sinem Aslan, Doug Doblar, Pratima Dutta, Yeol Huh, Dabae Lee, Kurt Richter, Sunnie Lee Watson, and Bill Watson for their input on early versions of the manuscript. We also appreciate Doug Thomas of Edvisions Schools, Bob Crumley of Chugach School District, and Kathy Frick of Bloomington Montessori School for vetting our information about their school systems. Many thanks to Minkyoung Kim for her work on the book cover. Finally, we would like to thank Alvin Toffler and many other authors we have cited for their valuable insights about paradigm change in society and education systems.

1

The Case for a Fundamental Change

The U.S. education system is under fire for many reasons, including these problems:

- mediocre student performance in relation to other countries
- low scores on standardized tests for too many of our children and schools
- inadequate preparation of students for college
- substandard focus in STEM areas (science, technology, engineering, and math)
- great inequities in the quality of education for many disadvantaged children

Policymakers and educators have been trying for decades to solve these problems by reforming schools, with disappointing results. Their approach has been to make reforms that leave the basic structure of the education system intact. But could that very structure be the source of the problems?

MEETING THE NEEDS OF ONLY A FEW

We propose that most schools in the United States are not designed to meet the education needs of students. It's a bold claim, right? How can schools not be designed for learning? That's supposed to be their whole gig.

Consider the setup of our current system:

- All students in a class are essentially taught the same material at the same time. The rate of progress is tailored to the middle performers in the class.
- Slower students seldom master all the material being taught, creating learning gaps that compromise the future learning of these students.
- The primary purpose of tests is to compare students to each other, rather than to compare student performance to a standard of achievement.
- To avoid criticisms of "grade inflation," teachers often limit the amount of time a student has to take a test. This also makes it easier to distinguish brighter students from slower ones.
- Student report cards track courses and grades. They don't indicate what a student has actually learned—or still needs to learn.

Here's what people involved with schools have to say about this current state of affairs:[1]

Samantha, a bright high school student:

I get bored in school. I don't have any choice about what to learn. There are lots of things I want to learn, but I have to learn stupid stuff in school. I can't learn about things that are important to me [in school], so I use Google a lot at home. I just do enough in school to get by.

Jeremy, a failing middle school student:

I hate school. Some kids are mean to me. The only good thing is I get to see my friends [at school]. I don't get much of what my teachers talk about, and, like . . . well, I just tune out most of the time. My teachers don't care much about me.

Robert, a seventh grade teacher:

I became a teacher because of Mr. Parker, my seventh grade teacher. He cared about me and made me want to do well. I wished I had more teachers like him, so I decided to become a teacher. But I get really frustrated. It's hard to get to know my students because I have 124 of them, and I only see them for 40 minutes a day. Just when I begin to get to know my students well, they move on to eighth grade. Plus, I need to spend so much time preparing them for the standardized test that it's hard to do things that can really excite them and make a difference in their lives. I bring my work home, but I have two children now, and I feel torn between them and my students. I just feel burned out. A nine-to-five job sounds really good to me now, but this isn't a good time to be looking [for a job].

Sarah, a parent:

I have two children in school, a girl in first grade and a boy in fourth. My son does well with structure; he needs to be given specific tasks and deadlines, and then he does well. But I'm really worried about Alicia. She is in a world of her own. It takes her a long time to do anything. But she's really bright and creative. She reads a lot and knows how to add small numbers, but she doesn't like to be rushed. She likes to do things well and likes the satisfaction of finishing things. Her teacher is forcing her to hand in work before she can finish it, and Alicia gets very frustrated about this. I'm afraid she's going to start hating school. Worse yet, she'll begin to hate the idea of learning. Her teacher and principal are both very polite, but nothing has changed. I wish I could have more influence over the way my daughter is being taught.

Steven, a business leader:

I'm very concerned about our schools. I own a small pharmaceutical business, and the young people I hire tend to lack initiative and work ethic. I'm also disappointed in these employees' low ability to solve problems and work on teams. I've tried to address these problems with our school superintendent, but I can't get anything to change.

A state legislator:

Our schools need to be more competitive globally for our economy to be strong. Since schools aren't improving on their own, we need to force them to improve. We have set higher standards for them to meet, and we are holding their feet to the fire. But we've been doing this for six years now, and I'm worried that it just isn't working. I don't know what else we can do.

Clearly, today's schools aren't perfect, but what makes us think they are not designed to meet the education needs of students? For starters, consider one of the few things that practically everyone—educators, parents, and even students—agrees on: Children learn at different rates and in different ways, and individuals have different learning needs. Yet schools typically teach a predetermined, fixed amount of content in a set amount of time.

In this rigid group-learning structure, within each classroom, slower learners like Jeremy and Alicia are forced to move on before they have learned the content, so they waste a lot of time and accumulate gaps in their learning that make it more difficult for them to learn related content in the future. Meanwhile, faster learners like Samantha become bored to frustration and waste a great deal of valuable time waiting for the class to move on, instead of forging ahead to new topics and skills. Holding back quick learners while others catch up squanders talent that communities and businesses sorely need.

MEETING THE NEEDS OF ALL

To meet the needs of all students, an educational system must allow for continuous progress for all students. It must not force students to move on before they learn current material, and it must not hold back faster students while the rest of the class catches up. Schools could take a cue from the Boy Scouts, an organization that knows how to ensure that people master practical, real-world skills. Scouts work on a merit badge until they achieve it, and then they move on to the next merit badge. Individuals progress through ranks based on their achievements, not time.

Time-based student progress forces achievement to vary—forces some students to be left behind. Time is the constant, and learning is the variable. The alternative is *attainment*-based student progress in which learning is the constant and time becomes the variable. This approach gives each student the amount of time needed to reach the standard for competency. A system designed for learning has the following characteristics:

- It does not force a student to move on *before* a certain standard is met.
- It allows a student to move on *as soon as* the standard is met.

This is a huge (bold!) difference—a *paradigm change*. And it is a change to a *true* standards-based approach to education, in contrast to a system that expects all students to reach the same standard at the same time.

DEATH OF THE CARNEGIE UNIT

The Carnegie Unit, also called the credit hour, was established in the early 1900s as a standard measure of student learning. One unit represents 120 hours of class or contact time with a teacher at the secondary level. The Carnegie Unit is the standard for all course credit in schools and universities. While it is intended to indicate amount of student learning, it really measures seat time.

The Carnegie Foundation for the Advancement of Teaching, which conceived the unit, received funding in 2012 to explore ways other than time to measure competency.

This funded project is an important indicator of growing recognition of the need to change from time-based student progress to learning-based progress. Furthermore, replacing the Carnegie Unit with a true measure of learning could do much to accelerate the transformation of education to a design for learning.

WHAT IS A *PARADIGM?*

The term "paradigm" applies to all sorts of topics, including the following examples:

Lighting: Paradigms of lighting include the flame (candles and whale oil lamps), the electric light bulb, and the light emitting diode (LED).

Transportation: Paradigms include foot travel, boats, horses, railroads, automobiles, and airplanes.

Family: Family paradigms include the tribal family, the extended family, the nuclear family, the single-parent family, and the dual-income family.

Education: Paradigms of education include the one-room schoolhouse, the current time-based factory model of schools, and the attainment-based system.

Piecemeal change: This is a change within a single paradigm, whereas *paradigm change* is change from one paradigm to another.

Although this learning-focused paradigm represents a bold change for schools in the United States, it's probably familiar to most people—not just the Boy Scouts. It's the way people naturally learn. This is the structure used in computer gaming, in which players must keep working on one level until they master it and unlock the next level. Mastering one level before moving on to a more difficult level makes sense. Moving on before mastery is a recipe for failure, but it is an inherent part of the structure of the current time-based paradigm of education. If we truly want our schools to reach and teach every child, then every child needs the opportunity to master a skill at one level before moving on to the next level of complexity.

PREPARING STUDENTS FOR OUTDATED BUSINESS NEEDS

Some people blame teachers for the problems in today's elementary and high schools: "Those darn unions are standing in the way of good education." Others blame school leaders: "We just need a better principal in charge here." Some blame parents: "Parents aren't disciplining their kids or making them do homework." Still others blame students: "They're lazy and don't care."

A close and thoughtful look may reveal that the lion's share of blame belongs to the *structure of the system*, not to its people. For an educational system to adequately prepare students to succeed in the world in which they live, the system must reflect the realities of the society in which it's operating.

Our current *paradigm* of schooling is often called the "factory model" and was developed for the Industrial Age, from about 1830 to 1960, when factory work had replaced farm work as the most common means for earning an income in the United States.

Think about the time long before factories, during the Hunting and Gathering Age, when a whole tribe was responsible for educating young people to improve their odds of survival. Then consider the change that occurred in the Agrarian Age, when most people lived and worked on farms. The one-room schoolhouse, along with tutorial instruction and apprenticeship, replaced that early form of education. Children needed basic math and reading skills to function in a farming community. There were no grade levels, no courses, no standardized tests. The community needed a learning-based system, not lockstep instruction on a fixed timetable. Older kids often helped younger ones.

WAVES OF CHANGE IN SOCIETIES

Alvin Toffler identified three major waves of change that triggered huge paradigm change in all sectors of society:

The *Agricultural Revolution* transformed society from hunting and gathering to agriculture.

The *Industrial Revolution* transformed society from agriculture to manufacturing.

The *Information Revolution* transformed society from manufacturing to knowledge work.

Toffler describes how each wave has brought huge changes to all aspects of life, including what he calls the techno-sphere (which produces and allocates wealth), socio-sphere (allocates roles to individuals), info-sphere (allocates information to make the other spheres work), and power-sphere (exercises power).

Education has changed paradigm with every one of these societal changes.

Now consider the Industrial Age. In transportation systems, railroads replaced boats for most transportation of goods, and horses gave way to cars. In the workplace, factory jobs surpassed farming jobs in number. In communications, the telegraph, telephone, and radio replaced the town crier and pony express. And in education systems, the one-room schoolhouse transformed into the age- and grade-specific factory model of schools that is still being used today.

To prepare children for factory jobs, schools needed to teach students to comply with instructions and discipline. The most important lessons were not part of the explicit curriculum; they were the "hidden curriculum"—what Alvin Toffler, author of *The Third Wave*, calls the "covert curriculum." Here are the lessons related to this curriculum:

- *Obedience*: Do what you're told to do (sit down and be quiet).
- *Punctuality*: Complete your tasks on time.
- *Stamina*: Get used to doing boring, repetitive tasks.
- *Standardization*: Get on pace with your peers to learn the same things in the same way at the same time.

In the Industrial Age, most people worked on assembly lines doing mindless tasks over and over again. Employers didn't need or want employees to have refined thinking skills. Therefore, educating all students to high levels was unnecessary and undesirable; it was also too expensive for most public education systems.

What employers did need was for the education system to prepare the majority of students for factory jobs and filter a smaller percentage of students to prepare to go on to higher education and become managers and professionals. The Industrial Age educational system was a great fit; it efficiently sorted students, separating those suited for manual labor from those more naturally suited for management or professional work.

In essence the Industrial Age paradigm was designed to leave many children behind. We can never succeed at NCLB as long as we keep the Industrial Age paradigm of education, with its time-based student progress that forces many students to move on before they really learn the material (i.e., master the standards).

The sorting function is also served by the grading system. Teachers often grade "on a curve" and thereby adjust student test grades depending on how well the group performs on the test. This means some students get As and others get Fs, regardless of the grade that the actual percentage of correct and incorrect answers warrant. This is known as "norm-referenced" testing in some circles (see Paradigms of Testing box).

PARADIGMS OF TESTING

Norm-referenced tests are intended to compare students with each other. A grade indicates how well a student performed compared to the other students in a class. Therefore, a B in biology may represent a very different level of performance in one school versus another.

In contrast, *criterion-referenced* tests are intended to validate that a student has reached a certain standard of competency. Grades indicate how much material on a topic a student learned.

At the dawn of the Industrial Age, complete paradigm change in education happened because communities changed dramatically—from a focus on farming to a focus on factories—and this caused a fundamental change in educational needs, including the hidden curriculum and higher levels of literacy and numeracy skills.

The United States is now a postindustrial society that is different in fundamental ways from an industrial society. Are these differences so dramatic that they have created another fundamental change in our educational needs? If so, then once again, we would need a *paradigm* change in education.

EXPLORING THE ESSENCE OF THE INFORMATION AGE

The work and educational needs of a nation during the Industrial Age were shaped by the prevailing technology of the time: machinery. Key characteristics of the Industrial Age include standardization, uniformity, adversarial relationships, bureaucracy, autocratic leadership, control, compliance, professional service, and compartmentalization. We explore each of these characteristics in this section and point out how they're different in today's information-based society—and what the changes mean for education and preparation for life.

Standardization to Customization

At the height of the Industrial Age, when the United States had the most workers in factories, our society was dominated by mass production (the assembly line), mass communication (newspapers, radio, television stations), and mass marketing (advertising via mass communications). Standardization was the name of the game.

REDEFINING THE ACHIEVEMENT GAP

The achievement gap is generally thought of as the gap between high- and low-performing students. This reflects industrial age thinking in which the intent is for all students to achieve the same competencies at the same time. Given that students learn at different rates, this inevitably requires holding back faster learners.

In information age thinking, the achievement gap is about the difference between how much a student is learning and how much that student *could* be learning. The highest goal for equity is to help all students reach their potential. That is the way to truly "leave no child behind."

Henry Ford commented about the Model T, "You can have any color you want, as long as it's black." Now, however, the Information Age is epitomized by Pandora's personalized radio that customizes songs based on each listener's preferences. Customers today demand custom products to meet their individual needs and preferences. Cell phones, Facebook, and Twitter offer increasingly powerful tools for customized communications. "Cookies" in your Internet browser give companies powerful insight for customizing marketing. In every facet of our lives today and across every industry, standardization has given way to customization.

Yet schools are seldom based on customization. Students in the same class are typically required to learn the same things at the same time and rate. Also, all teachers have typically received the same professional development at the same time, regardless of whether they had already learned it or whether the training was relevant to their needs (though this has begun to change as our society evolves deeper into the Information Age). Standardized tests tend to assess all students in a given grade on the same competencies at the same time. For the most part, public elementary schools and high schools in the United States are still standardized, not customized.

Uniformity to Diversity

At the height of the Industrial Age in the 1930s and 1940s, most people tried to blend in. If you look at a picture of a busy city street at this time, you see that many people dressed the same way, drove cars that looked the same (the black Model T!), and had the same kind of haircut. But this isn't how groups of people look and behave anymore! Now you see tremendous variation in the way people dress, what they drive, and how they wear their hair.

Uniformity has given way to diversity in most aspects of life, particularly in academic and workplace situations. Employers now see diversity of perspectives and skills as a huge advantage.

Similarly, the student mix in today's classrooms is more diverse than ever; thus, individuals in a classroom learn in ever more different ways and rates. That's okay, because the job market requires people to have many more different kinds of skills. Yet, for the most part, even with the recent interest in differentiated instruction and response to intervention (RTI), public elementary schools and high schools in the United States still focus on uniformity. Rather than embracing and promoting diversity, teachers expect all students in a class to learn the same things at the same rate.

Adversarial to Collaborative Relationships

People often think of competition as the alternative to collaboration. However, it is not competition that's giving way to collaboration in today's communities. Competition is neither less important nor less common in the Information Age than it was in earlier times. If anything, competition is intensified by global markets and a greater variety of choices for consumers. But *adversarial relationships* are giving way to collaborative relationships for success in the Information Age.

For example, in the Industrial Age, labor strikes were common; relationships between workers and employers were typically adversarial. Labor strikes are much less common now. Since knowledge work has replaced manual labor as the most common form of work, companies are recognizing that their most valuable asset is the knowledge that their employees possess. Competent knowledge workers are more difficult to replace, so companies are increasingly investing in their employees' professional development, building trust, and treating employees well. In 2010 alone, private companies spent $52.8 billion on employee training.[2]

Adversarial relationships were also common in schools during the Industrial Age. Teacher strikes were fairly common then, and the relationships between teachers and students were—and still are—typically perceived (by many students at least) as adversarial, as captured in movies like *Ferris Bueller's Day Off* and song lyrics like "Hey, teacher, leave those kids alone." In fact, some teachers even purposely withhold information from students to see who can figure out answers on their own.

Sheer class size also abets the adversarial vibe. High school teachers typically have 100–150 students in a semester that they see in batches of 25–30 for about forty minutes a day. The inherent anonymity that this situation fosters means adversarial (instead of collaborative) relationships prevail.

And what about the relationship between teachers and parents? They're often adversarial, too, in the Industrial Age education system, especially student-teacher and teacher-administrator relationships. Many parents feel unwelcome in their children's schools, and many teachers feel frustrated with parents' lack of involvement or support, though this is beginning to change in some schools. Finally, the relationship between school boards and administrators is often adversarial as well in the current system. Many school boards demonstrate a lack of faith in administrators by micromanaging through strict oversight.

Some of these Industrial Age features are beginning to change in some places, but unfortunately many school systems nationwide are still generally characterized by adversarial relationships—not the more productive collaborative ones. Education systems will become increasingly dysfunctional until the core relationships among students, teachers, parents, administrators, and governing bodies transform from adversarial to collaborative.

Bureaucracy to Teams

Bureaucracy was the most common organizational structure for decision making in the Industrial Age. But bureaucracy tends to be very slow to make decisions because it takes time for information to work its way up the various levels of a bureaucracy and for decisions to then work their way down to the "front lines." But, really, this system worked fine when the pace of change was relatively slow. That's not the case in today's world of round-the-clock, instant communication. The Information Age brought rapid change to the marketplace, so companies that respond slowly are at a potentially fatal competitive disadvantage. To become more agile, companies are forming relatively autonomous teams that have latitude to make their own decisions but are held accountable for their performance.

Similarly, the Industrial Age paradigm of education was (and still is) characterized by consolidation into large school districts managed by bureaucracies. This makes it difficult for teachers to respond rapidly to the changing needs of the increasingly diverse students in their classrooms. Movements toward site-based management, shared decision making, and team teaching reflect a growing recognition of the need for our bureaucratic education systems to take a page from the business world's playbook and transform into team-based organizations.

Autocratic to Shared Leadership

Bureaucratic organization tends to be autocratic or dictatorial. This structure assumes that the people at the top of the bureaucracy are the most qualified individuals to make good decisions for the entire organization. And this worked fine when frontline workers were performing very simple jobs, but that's no longer the case. For complex and rapidly changing knowledge work, frontline workers are often the most qualified individuals to make critical decisions about product design, production, and marketing. Shared decision making and leadership can put some organizations at a significant advantage over their more traditionally structured counterparts.

Similarly, in the world of education, with an increasingly diverse student population, an ever more complex array of technological tools to support learning, and a growing need to customize learning experiences for students, shared decision making is the way to go. Teachers, parents, and students themselves can benefit as never before from being part of decisions about teaching and learning.

Centralized Control to Autonomy with Accountability

Bureaucratic organization, autocratic leadership, and standardization are all powerful tools for centralized control, and they are all systemically related to, and supportive of, each other. This *interdependence* of key characteristics is inherent to any paradigm. But one can have bureaucracy and autocratic leadership in autonomous units. So this is a different characteristic from the others, though it's related. The growing problem is that centralized control in large systems requires bureaucracy, and bureaucratic organization works too slowly to deal effectively with the increasingly rapid rate of change.

Team-based organization requires distributed control, or *autonomy*, but teams must be accountable for their performance. According to Thomas Malone, a shift is occurring in the workplace from "command and control" to "coordinate and cultivate." You can get a sense for what this means by thinking about corporate restructuring efforts that eliminate middle levels of management and replace layers of centralized control with teams that have a large degree of autonomy and accountability for their performance.

U.S. public education systems are still characterized by centralized control. The larger the system, the more centralized the control. But different schools in a large district tend to have very different demographics and thus different kinds of students with different needs. Equity used to be thought of as treating all students the same, but now with high levels of diversity, equity requires people to treat students according to their needs. Centralized control does not promote flexibility for educators to treat students differently according to individual needs. The movements toward site-based management, shared decision making, and charter schools all reflect some recognition of a need for schools to have more autonomy for the means and be held to greater accountability for results.

Compliance to Initiative

In the Industrial Age, it was important for those working on an assembly line to follow directions. Compliance was an important part of the "hidden curriculum" in schools. Students were expected to sit down, be quiet, and do what they were told to do; students who didn't behave according to these expectations did not succeed in this education system.

A school board member who was the founder of a tool company in Richmond, Indiana, mentioned that he used to be able to hire a high school dropout, show him how to use a lathe, and know the employee would probably work out well. Now, he said, he needs to hire people who can work well in quality circles and have good communication and problem-solving skills.[3] He needs employees who take initiative to solve problems and improve processes, not people who wait around to be told what to do.

Changing the hidden curriculum of our schools from compliance to self-direction and initiative requires fundamental changes in the structure of educational systems.

Professional Service to Self Service

In the Industrial Age, an attendant pumped your gas, a porter carried your suitcases, an accountant prepared your taxes, and so forth. Now technology makes it easy to pump your own gas, wheel your own suitcases, prepare your own taxes, check out your own groceries, conduct banking transactions, and much more. Self-service has become the norm in many spheres. Similarly, Alvin Toffler wrote about the "prosumer" in the Information Age as someone who is simultaneously the producer and consumer of a good or service. For example, Wikipedia is a kind of user-produced encyclopedia. It is updated by users and available to all—for free.

In education, learning is still overwhelmingly "delivered" by professionals (teachers), even though the Internet in general and Google in particular have made self-serve learning much quicker, easier, and less expensive than even the do-it-yourself books that became so common just a few decades ago. *Open educational resources* are free, self-serve, learning tools on the Internet that enable people to learn almost anything. The availability of no-cost valuable resources has huge implications for education, but these tools are frequently unavailable for use in today's schools. Most schools greatly restrict Internet access, and most limit students to a small set of websites on a small number of computers available at limited times.

Compartmentalization to Holism

A common characteristic of bureaucratic organizations is division into departments. Businesses typically have departments for product development, production, marketing, sales, finance, and purchasing. Similarly, governments, hospitals, universities, and even large law firms are organized into departments. Local school districts follow this model, too. The central office has departments in large school districts, and even the content for learning is usually divided into subject areas (math, science, social studies), despite the interdisciplinary nature of the real world.

However, as business experts Michael Hammer and Michael Champy point out, corporations are finding that by "reengineering" their processes, they can significantly improve their efficiency and effectiveness. Process reengineering typically involves (1) creating a "case team" with members from each of those departments to cover all the skills needed, and (2) having the team conduct the entire process together. This greatly reduces the time, errors, rework, and expense for each performance of the entire process. Hammer and Champy found that a case-worker-based process (which is holistic) typically operates ten times faster than the assembly-line version it replaces (which is compartmentalized), and it also generates fewer errors.

Information Age schools have found several ways to reengineer the educational process for each student. One way is to create a case team made up of all students' teachers. Another is to have one teacher serve as a student's guide and mentor for all grade levels that are taught in the school. Examples of some of these innovations are included in chapter 3.

The Information Age is far more complex than the Industrial Age. This complexity applies to virtually all systems in society: the economy, governments, businesses, financial systems, healthcare systems, transportation systems, communications systems, and, yes, educational systems. Solving problems today requires an understanding of "system dynamics"; people need to know how things are interrelated. A holistic or systemic view of the world has huge advantages. Whereas compartmentalization was fine for a simpler, mechanical age, it does not get the job done today. Mechanistic thinking often entails an either/or (reductionist) perspective, but systemic thinking entails a both/and (expansionist) approach.

Table 1.1 lists some of the key differences between the Industrial Age and the Information Age. This side-by-side comparison highlights general ways the paradigm of education needs to change to meet the current needs of students, organizations, and communities.

Table 1.1. Comparison of Key Characteristics of Two Ages

Industrial Age	*Information Age*
Standardization	Customization
Uniformity	Diversity
Adversarial relationships	Collaborative relationships
Bureaucratic organization	Team organization
Autocratic leadership	Shared leadership
Centralized control	Empowerment, accountability
Compliance	Initiative and self-direction
Professional service	Self-service
Compartmentalization	Holism
(Division of labor)	(Integration of tasks)

CHANGING EDUCATIONAL NEEDS OF STUDENTS

The educational needs of students have been particularly influenced by the changes in the key characteristics shown in table 1.1. Here are some of the major changes in student needs:

1. *Knowledge work.* Manual labor has given way to knowledge work as the most common type of work today, just as manual labor replaced farm labor as the most common form of work during the Industrial Age. This means that many more students need to be highly educated today versus fifty years ago for the United States to compete with knowledge workers in other parts of the world, including India and China. In 2004, the United States graduated about 70,000 undergraduate engineers, compared to India's 350,000 and China's 600,000. In a "flat" world in which graduates compete with knowledge workers globally, only those who are best prepared for knowledge work will have the best standards of living.
2. *Complexity.* Everything has become more complex than it was in the Industrial Age or Agrarian Age. Financial systems, communication systems, and even entertainment systems are more complex now than they were in the past. Just try going into a friend's house and using their TV! Performing in today's world requires much higher levels of education—and a different kind of education (such as higher-order thinking and problem-solving skills)—than it did in the Industrial Age.
3. *Systemic thinking.* Systemic thinking and understanding the dynamic interrelationships within various systems are important for effective civic education, yet the current educational system decontextualizes

and compartmentalizes the real world into discrete subject areas without addressing their powerful interrelationships. For example, many factors influence how much oil we consume in the United States: the international price of oil, how cold the weather is, automobile mileage requirements, attitudes about global warming, availability of alternative energy sources, taxes on oil consumption, and much more. Focusing on any single aspect of this issue reveals a flawed and incomplete picture.

4. *Diversity of skills.* Whereas teaching everyone the same things served people well in the Industrial Age, developing students with the same set of skills no longer makes sense for a job market that requires so many different kinds of knowledge and skills. Cultivating students' individual talents will better meet their needs and their communities' needs than forcing them all to try to learn the same things. This is different from sorting students, because sorting entails teaching all students the same things at the same rate, so slower students flunk out. Here, students are taught different things, depending on their talents and interests. Of course, much common knowledge is still important.

5. *Collaboration.* Businesses and other organizations need employees who can work well with others on a team, communicate well, and resolve conflicts. Part of the hidden curriculum in the Industrial Age was "don't collaborate; that's cheating." It was tough to compare students if they helped each other learn. In the Information Age, the hidden curriculum must foster collaboration.

6. *Initiative.* Employers need people who take initiative to identify and solve problems, even in manufacturing environments. Part of the hidden curriculum in the Industrial Age paradigm is "sit down, be quiet, and do what you're told to do." Compliance is the goal. That made sense in the Industrial Age, because companies needed compliance on the assembly line and in the bureaucratic hierarchy. But knowledge workers need initiative and self-direction.

Given these new educational needs, *everyone* needs higher levels of education to attain a good quality of life. A school system that's designed for sorting students is no longer making the grade. Now, a complete focus on learning is critical for ensuring that every child reaches his potential, rather than relegating a majority of children to a narrow range of opportunities. Schools that foster systemic thinking, problem solving, diverse skill development, collaboration, and initiative are far better suited to prepare students to be happy and productive in today's complex and competitive world than is the current paradigm.

But don't take our word for it. These new needs are so great that multinational corporations and educational organizations came together in the Partnership for 21st Century Skills to identify ways of meeting the new needs. In addition, studies by the Department of Labor (the Secretary's Commission on Achieving Necessary Skills), the National Center on Education and the Economy (New Commission on the Skills of the American Workforce), and the National School Boards Association's Center for Public Education agree that these new kinds of skills are essential for all in U.S. society today.

Piecemeal reforms in our education systems are the norm, the go-to action, making it easy to overlook paradigm change, a kind of change that is unfamiliar and more challenging. During the Hunting and Gathering Age, the paradigm was education by the whole tribe ("it takes a village to raise a child"). During the Agrarian Age it was the one-room schoolhouse and apprenticeship or tutorial instruction. During the Industrial Age it's been the factory model of schools. Each of these paradigms has its own key characteristics that served the world in which it operated.

From this larger perspective, it stands to reason that *paradigm change must and will eventually take place in education* as we move deeper into the Information Age. An outdated educational system cannot adequately prepare students to succeed in the real world no matter:

- how much money is invested in training teachers to perform outdated techniques;
- how high the stakes become for students to perform on standardized tests;
- how low the student-to-teacher ratio becomes;
- how much competition is inflicted on public schools by charter schools and vouchers; and
- how much technology is integrated into classrooms.

A system designed to hold back the brightest students, leave behind those who need more time, and prepare all students for a world that no longer exists cannot continue to be the predominant paradigm of education.

Examples of the Information Age paradigm of education do already exist (see chapter 3); they're just not yet the most common paradigm, and they need further development.

Understanding the S-Curve and Paradigm Change

Paradigms have a common pattern of development known as the "S-curve," so it's possible to see where the new paradigm of education stands. This may seem a bit technical, but knowing about the S-Curve helps to see the nature and challenges of paradigm change, which are very different from those of piecemeal reforms.

Paradigms in the Industrial Age were considerably more complex than in the Agrarian Age, and those in the Information Age are more complex than they were in the Industrial Age. For communication systems, the Internet and cell phones are far more complex than radio and the telephone, which in turn are more complex than the pony express. And for education, the learner-centered paradigm is far more complex than the current factory model, which in turn is more complex than the one-room schoolhouse.

All types of systems evolve to ever-greater complexity: biological, communication, transportation, education, and so forth. This evolution of *classes* of systems (paradigms) to ever-greater complexity counterbalances the process of decay of *individual* systems into simpler components (called entropy); it's the yin and yang of all systems in the universe, the creative force and the destructive force. For example, retailing organizations have become considerably more complex in the Information Age, with companies like Amazon and Costco using complex operations and advanced technologies. While retailing has evolved to much greater complexity, individual companies that have not evolved have died off, such as Woolworth and Service Merchandise.

So how does a system develop? Consider the airplane. When it was first developed, it couldn't do much in terms of today's important criteria such as speed, comfort, distance, payload, safety, and reliability. But over time, piecemeal changes gradually improved the performance of this machine. There was a period when the improvements came at a rapid pace, and then they tapered off as the airplane essentially reached its upper limit for performance.

You can see this pattern of development in figure 1.1; it's typically called an "S-curve." Performance of a new system starts out way below its potential

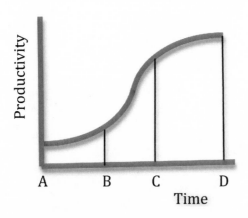

Figure 1.1. An S-curve for System Development Shows Piecemeal Change

(its upper limit), gradually improves at first (from time A to time B in figure 1.1), then undergoes a period of rapid improvement (from time B to time C), and finally tapers off as it approaches its upper limit (time C to time D). Improvements along a single S-curve are called *piecemeal changes* or *reforms*.

When the Industrial Age paradigm of education was first developed to replace the one-room schoolhouse (time A in figure 1.1), it was only able to achieve a relatively low level of student learning compared to what students learned in the 1950s (time C in figure 1.1). Educational reforms were highly effective from the 1930s to the 1950s (from time B to time C). But, over the past four decades, reforms have failed to improve educational outcomes of the overall system. This indicates that the Industrial Age paradigm of education has come so close to its upper limit that even significant investments (of effort and money) on reforms cannot produce the desired improvements in system performance.

To improve performance beyond the upper limit of a system, we must turn to a *different paradigm* that has a higher upper limit. The railroad was the most common paradigm of transportation for most of the Industrial Age, reaching its upper limit in the 1950s.[4] Achieving improvements beyond that upper limit required the development of a different paradigm, the airplane, as an alternative to the railroad. A new paradigm is represented by a new S-curve, which begins at a relatively low level of productivity (time E in figure 1.2). The airplane's initial performance was lower than the performance of the railroad at time E, but its upper limit (time G), in terms of speed and

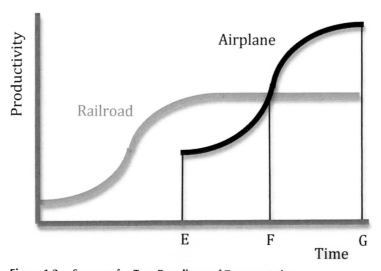

Figure 1.2. S-curves for Two Paradigms of Transportation

distance, safety, and other criteria, is considerably higher than that of the railroad.

In the world of education, "research-based methods of instruction" seem to be getting all the love recently, but the S-curve shows that research could (mis)lead us to abandon a promising new paradigm if, in its early stages of development, it does not match up to an older paradigm. Any research that compared the airplane to the railroad before time F would have led us to abandon it as a "research-based method" of transportation, yet the focus of educational reform today is on research-based methods.

The S-curve story indicates that the Industrial Age paradigm of education has reached its upper limit. Sure, we can improve an *individual* poor-performing school with piecemeal changes, such as replacing less effective educators with more effective ones, but this lowers performance in the schools where those effective teachers come from, so the system overall doesn't improve. Even if we double the investment per child throughout the current educational system, we would, at best, achieve a small improvement in student learning overall.

But has the Information Age paradigm of education reached the point where it outperforms the factory model of schools (time F in figure 1.2)? The schools described in chapter 3 and the many others listed in appendix A provide some evidence that the answer is "yes," particularly in terms of measures other than standardized tests, including creativity, initiative, collaboration skills, and responsibility. Therefore, we suggest that any future investments in education are best spent implementing the Information Age paradigm of education and conducting research and development (R&D) to improve it.

CHAPTER SUMMARY OF KEY IDEAS

Efforts to reform the current education system have not been successful. Most schools today are designed more for sorting students than for ensuring learning for all students.

- Time-based student progress forces slower learners to move on before learning the material, wasting time, and creating learning gaps that make future learning more difficult.
- Time-based student progress forces faster learners to wait to move on after learning the material, wasting time, and triggering boredom and frustration.

Education must be designed for student learning, which calls for a different paradigm.

- Student progress must be based on amount of learning (meeting standards), not on the amount of time spent in school or on a specific subject.
- An attainment-based, continuous-progress education system requires new roles for teachers, students, technology, and even parents.

Many schools in today's education system are designed to leave some children behind.

- The blame belongs to the system, not its people.
- The one-room schoolhouse was the predominant paradigm of education during the Agrarian Age.
- The factory model of schools was the predominant education paradigm during the Industrial Age, when factory labor was predominant, and schools needed to teach students obedience, punctuality, stamina, and standardization, and students were sorted into groups of potential managers or laborers.
- Sorting students is the purpose of norm-referenced student assessment.
- A new paradigm of education is needed and inevitable for the Information Age.

Paradigms have been changing.

- The key characteristics of the Information Age tend to be polar opposites of those of the Industrial Age, and these characteristics represent the deep structure of all societal systems.
- Key characteristics of Information Age systems include customization, diversity, collaboration, team-based organizational structures, shared leadership, empowerment with accountability, initiative or self-direction, self-service, and holism or systems thinking. These help us to envision the new paradigm of education.

The United States has new needs for its education system.

- Knowledge work has replaced factory labor as the predominant form of work, and knowledge work requires higher levels of education for most students than factory labor used to.
- Many aspects of life are now far more complex, and navigating the everyday world requires higher levels of education and thinking for everyone.
- Interrelationships and causal dynamics influence decisions in all aspects of life; understanding this is helpful.

- Diversity of skills is critical for a specialized division of labor, and it requires an educational system that cultivates individual talents of all kinds.
- U.S. citizens must know how to collaborate, communicate well, and resolve conflicts to succeed in modern life.
- People who take initiative to identify and solve problems are more valuable in today's workforce than those who wait to follow orders; people develop initiative through self-directed learning.
- Piecemeal reforms cannot adequately address the new set of student needs; an entirely new education paradigm is required and inevitable.

The S-curve helps for understanding paradigm change.

- Systems evolve to ever-greater complexity.
- The development of any one system is typically characterized by an S-curve, eventually reaching its upper limit and requiring a new paradigm to make further improvements in performance.
- The factory model of schools reached its upper limit a while ago, and further investments in improving it continue to yield disappointing results.
- Investments in education are much better spent to develop the Information Age paradigm rather than pouring money into an outdated model.

NOTES

1. These individuals and statements represent the views expressed by multiple people that we've compiled into these summaries.

2. www.nwlink.com/~donclark/hrd/trainsta.html

3. A quality circle is a volunteer group composed of workers (or even students), usually under the leadership of their supervisor (or an elected team leader), who are trained to identify, analyze, and solve work-related problems and present solutions to management to improve the performance of the organization and to motivate and enrich the work of employees.

4. A new paradigm of a subsystem can raise a system's upper limit, such as the jet engine for the airplane. The high-speed railway has increased the upper limit of the railroad beyond that of the 1950s.

RELATED READINGS

Ackoff, Russell L. *Creating the Corporate Future*. New York: Wiley, 1981.

Banathy, Bela H. *Systems Design of Education: A Journey to Create the Future*. Englewood Cliffs, NJ: Educational Technology Publications, 1991.

Branson, Robert K. "Why the Schools Can't Improve: The Upper Limit Hypothesis." *Journal of Instructional Development* 10, no. 4 (1987): 15–26.

Christensen, Clayton M., Michael B. Horn, and Curtis W. Johnson. *Disrupting Class: How Disruptive Innovation Will Change the Way the World Learns.* New York: McGraw-Hill, 2008.

Darling-Hammond, Linda. "Achieving Our Goals: Superficial or Structural Reforms." *Phi Delta Kappan* 72, no. 4 (1990): 286–95.

Department of Labor. *What Work Requires of Schools: A SCANS Report for America 2000.* Washington, DC: U.S. Department of Labor, 1991. Available at wdr.doleta .gov/SCANS/whatwork/

Friedman, Thomas L. *The World Is Flat: A Brief History of the Twenty-first Century.* New York: Farrar, Straus and Giroux, 2005.

Hammer, Michael, and James Champy. *Reengineering the Corporation: A Manifesto for Business Revolution.* New York: HarperBusiness, 2001.

KnowledgeWorks Foundation. "2020 Forecast: Creating the Future of Learning." Cincinnati, OH: KnowledgeWorks Foundation, 2012.

Malone, Thomas W. *The Future of Work.* Boston: Harvard Business School Press, 2004.

Naisbitt, John, and Patricia Aburdene. *Megatrends 2000: Ten New Directions for the 1990's.* New York: William Morrow and Company, 1990.

National Education Commission on Time and Learning, *Prisoners of Time.* Washington, DC: National Education Commission on Time and Learning. Available at www2.ed.gov/pubs/PrisonersOfTime/index.html.

Reigeluth, Charles M. "Educational Standards: To Standardize or to Customize Learning?" *Phi Delta Kappan* 79, no. 3 (1997): 202–6.

Reigeluth, Charles M., and Robert J. Garfinkle. *Systemic Change in Education.* Englewood Cliffs, NJ: Educational Technology Publications, 1994.

Schlechty, Phillip C. *Shaking up the School House.* San Francisco: Jossey-Bass, 2001.

Senge, Peter M. *Schools That Learn: A Fifth Discipline Fieldbook for Educators, Parents, and Everyone Who Cares about Education.* New York: Doubleday, 2000.

Sturgis, Chris, Susann Patrick, and Linda Pittenger. *It's Not a Matter of Time: Highlights from the 2011 Competency-Based Learning Summit.* Vienna, VA: iNACOL, 2011. Available at www.inacol.org/research/competency/index.php.

Toffler, Alvin. *The Third Wave.* New York: Bantam Books, 1980.

———. *Powershift.* New York: Bantam Books, 1990.

Tyack, David B., and Larry Cuban. *Tinkering toward Utopia: A Century of Public School Reform.* Cambridge, MA: Harvard University Press, 1995.

Wagner, Tony. *Making the Grade: Reinventing America's Schools.* New York: RoutledgeFalmer, 2002.

Wheatley, Margaret J. *Leadership and the New Science: Discovering Order in a Chaotic World.* San Francisco: Berrett-Koehler Publishers, 1999.

RELATED WEBSITES

The American Association of School Administrators: www.aasa.org

The International Association for K–12 Online Learning: www.inacol.org

The National Center on Education and the Economy, New Commission on the Skills of the American Workforce: www.skillscommission.org

The National School Boards Association's Center for Public Education: www.centerforpubliceducation.org

The Partnership for 21st Century Skills: www.21stcenturyskills.org/

The Secretary's Commission on Achieving Necessary Skills: wdr.doleta.gov/SCANS/whatwork/

2

A Vision of Information Age Education

A learning-focused, attainment-based education paradigm can be implemented inexpensively and well in a school environment. Some places in which this paradigm is already being used are described in chapter 3. But fully implementing a new paradigm requires a massive change in how people look at the role of education overall and the roles of teachers, students, parents, administrators, and even technology. As Phillip Schlechty, a national leader in fundamental change, says, "It requires big changes in the way schools use time, talent, and technology."

The new paradigm of education must meet the educational needs of a school district's community, its state-level educational system, and our society in general (its "systemic environment"). If it doesn't meet those needs, the

TEACHERS: DO YOUR TEACHING PRACTICES ALIGN WITH YOUR CORE BELIEFS ABOUT TEACHING AND LEARNING?

Did you, like most teachers, go into teaching because you wanted to make a positive difference in children's lives? Did you believe you could help every child learn, help each to enjoy learning, and inspire each to learn more?

Are you reaching these goals? If not, what is keeping you from reaching them? Perhaps it is the "system"—the industrial age paradigm. Try to imagine a system that would allow you to reach your goals. What core ideas would it have?

systemic environment will not support the new school system—with money or students or both. The educational needs of the community include those of its students, parents, employers, government, service organizations, retired citizens, and many more.

Therefore, an accurate vision of the new education paradigm must be based on today's educational needs and the key characteristics for the Information Age (described in chapter 1).

In this chapter, we propose six core ideas that focus on student learning rather than student sorting and provide a solid foundation for schools in the Information Age paradigm. This will place the focus of schools primarily on *learning* to better meet the needs of students and their communities in the modern world. The six core ideas are:

1. attainment-based system
2. learner-centered instruction
3. expanded curriculum that includes twenty-first-century skills
4. new roles for teachers, students, parents, and technology
5. nurturing school culture
6. organizational structures, choice, incentive, and decision-making systems

When these core ideas are implemented, schools in the new paradigm will differ far more from each other than schools do currently. After all, diversity is a key characteristic of the Information Age. Therefore, the core ideas may be implemented in many different ways in the new paradigm.

Furthermore, the new paradigm will better prepare students for the modern world and be more cost-effective than our current paradigm, for reasons we point out at the end of this chapter.

The vision we describe in this chapter is intended to stimulate thinking about what's possible for education, rather than to present a full solution. All aspects presented are not necessary—or even advisable—for every community or school. We present this vision simply to inspire your imagination to see how the U.S. public school system may transcend the factory model that's now in play.

CORE IDEA 1: ATTAINMENT-BASED SYSTEM

For an education system to be focused primarily on learning, student progress must be based on learning, not time. This means that student assessment and records must indicate what a student has actually learned, rather than comparing her to other students.

Student Progress

When this core idea is operating, each student moves on to a new topic or competency only after demonstrating proficiency through a fixed and credible standard of achievement—not when a fixed amount of time has passed or when other students hit certain achievement milestones. A student is not forced to move on before reaching the proficiency standard, and each student moves on as soon as the standard is reached. This is a standards-based approach to education in a true sense of the term, and this core idea is vital to maximum student learning.

Testing

The twin purposes of student evaluation are to guide student learning (known as *formative assessment*) and to validate student achievement (which is *summative assessment*). *Norm-referenced assessment* is what we have in today's education system, and it serves to compare students with each other. Norm-referenced assessment is not used in the Information Age paradigm.

Formative assessment (also covered in the upcoming "Learner-Centered Instruction" section) provides each student with immediate feedback on performance, with hints and other forms of guidance to help the student learn from her successes and failures. Summative assessment validates a student's competency at a certain level or standard. These performance-based assessments are fully integrated with instruction, so no time is taken away from learning for testing.

In the Information Age paradigm we envision, all students are expected to finish learning whatever they undertake to learn. In other words, all learning continues until it is successful. Each summative assessment is based on a single competency (or a small set of them), rather than on a comprehensive basis or a large number of learning areas at once. This means there would never be a single large assessment to cover an entire school term. Further, these small assessments are integrated naturally and seamlessly with personalized instruction to certify as well as improve learning. This means that students take tests when they are ready for them, based on their individual learning needs and progress—not at a predetermined time established by the curriculum, administrators, politicians, or bureaucrats.

Student learning in the academic disciplines is assessed, and students are also expected to demonstrate an understanding of how to apply cross-discipline knowledge in a series of real-world projects. This approach ensures that students have a solid grasp on the essentials while also pushing them to apply their learning to various contexts, which provides educators a more accurate picture of an individual's educational progress.

Report Cards

Results of summative assessments are entered into a record of attainments for each student. In a technology-based learning environment, this happens automatically when possible. When human judgment is needed, an expert observer can evaluate the student using a mobile device that contains an appropriate observation rubric.

Student records are automatically maintained and updated for teachers, and each attainment may be linked to a portfolio item that provides supporting documentation when appropriate. The Information Age report card contains no grades; instead, it contains lists or maps of attainments for which a student has met the standards of competency, as in the Khan Academy, which is a website that offers free use of a library with more than 3,800 videos on everything from arithmetic to history and hundreds of skills to practice with immediate feedback and built-in competency assessment and records of attainments.

Parents who want to compare their child with other children can compare levels of attainment instead of grades, but it's likely that any one student will be ahead of another in some areas and behind that same other student in other areas, reducing stigma for any given child. All children eventually succeed at all learning they undertake in the Information Age paradigm, which greatly enhances individual motivation and self-esteem.

CORE IDEA 2: LEARNER-CENTERED INSTRUCTION

An attainment-based system requires instruction to be customized to each student's learning needs rather than standardized. This creates benefits for using project-based learning, collaborative learning, instructional support, and the treatment of children with special needs.

Customized (or Personalized) Learning

Attainment-based student progress is one form of customization (*customized pacing*). But the Information Age paradigm goes beyond this to include *customized content* and *customized methods* as well.

Regarding content, all students in the Information Age paradigm are required to learn a core body of material, which usually entails focusing on deficits regarding the requirements (and thus is often called *deficit-based learning*). However, considerable time is also available for students to cultivate their individual talents, interests, and strengths (often called *asset-based learning*). In the Information Age system we envision, the best of both deficit- and asset-based approaches are applied, representing "both–and" rather than "either–or" thinking.

Regarding methods, Howard Gardner, who is famous for his work on multiple intelligences, has shown that students differ in their profile of eight major kinds of intelligence and has argued that a student's strongest intelligences can be used most effectively as "entry points" for learning new knowledge, skills, and attitudes. Consequently, methods are customized in two major ways: through student selection of projects and through customized tutorials (both are described later in this section). Project selection and tutorials are customized according to multiple intelligences, student interests, learning styles, and other kinds of learner characteristics and preferences.

Personal learning plans or *learning contracts* (different in important ways from individualized education plans [IEPs][1]) are essential planning and monitoring tools for customizing learning. The parents, mentor-teacher, and student meet on a regular basis (perhaps every two or three months) to establish a new plan or contract for the next period and to review the student's accomplishments on the previous plan. The parents and student have considerable input to specify the goals and outcomes in the plan, but the teacher, community, state, and even the nation have the right and obligation to assure (through monitoring) that appropriate standards are being met. However, there is considerable flexibility in deciding when which standards are met.

Means for how student goals will be met are also identified in the planning meeting, with parents and teacher assuming agreed-on roles in support of the student's efforts. This approach to creating and managing a personal learning plan can be implemented cost-effectively with the help of technology, as described in "Core Idea 3: New Roles" later in this chapter.

Project-Based Learning

To truly customize learning, students must be allowed to work on different tasks that are relevant to their individual interests and needs. Authentic projects (that is, projects that are real-world or similar to real-world) are powerful for customized learning because they enhance *intrinsic motivation*,[2] which is crucial to accelerating learning. Such projects also aid the transfer of learning to practical situations.

Well-designed tasks that are not authentic projects can also be powerful ways to customize learning, particularly for younger learners, as demonstrated in Montessori preschools (see chapter 4), where students are deeply engaged in performing a task over and over and over again—by choice. Mastery is a powerful motivator.

Most projects are interdisciplinary to be authentic and require a relatively long time to complete—days for younger students and weeks or months for older ones. Formative assessment, including guidance and coaching, is provided in projects, either by a teacher or by a technology system in a simulation or "virtual world," like *Second Life*. Summative assessment is conducted but doesn't offer much value for assessing individual learning in project work unless a student does the project alone.

Some projects are community-based service projects, others are conducted through computer-based simulations or virtual worlds, and still others use a combination of the two through use of mobile devices (another example of both–and thinking).

Collaborative Learning

In businesses, a great deal of knowledge work is done in teams. Collaboration is important in work life, civic life, and family life, and working with others provides extra motivation to students who enjoy a social dimension to learning. Collaboration also provides a valuable opportunity for students to learn from each other. Team-based learning pushes students to develop their teamwork and conflict-resolution skills with teacher guidance. However, students may occasionally choose to work independently on a project.

Instructional Support

As powerful as collaborative project-based learning is for motivation and real-world application of knowledge, we have found four shortcomings of team-based project work in our teaching experience:

1. A team typically produces a product, and the whole team is assessed on that product. This makes it difficult to ensure that all students learned the important project-related competencies. Sometimes a team has a loafer who doesn't learn much at all. Also, teammates often work co-operatively rather than collaboratively, meaning each person performs different tasks and therefore learns different things. In our experience, it is rare for any student to learn all the intended lessons of a project. For a system in which student progress is based on learning, it is important to accurately determine what each student on the team learns, but this is tough to do in project-based learning.
2. The skills and competencies available through projects are usually ones that learners need to transfer to a broad range of situations, especially for complex cognitive tasks. However, in project-based learning, stu-

dents typically use a skill only once or twice during the project. This makes it difficult for them to learn to use the skill in the full range of situations in which they are likely to need it in the future. Many skills require extensive practice to develop to a proficient or expert level, yet that rarely happens in project-based learning.

3. Some skills need to become automatic, or performed without thinking, to free up the student's conscious cognitive processing for higher-level thinking when executing a task. For example, when a person first learns to drive a car, he's usually so focused on the mechanics of driving that he cannot pay attention to more strategic issues of navigation and defensive driving tactics. After a while, the mechanics of driving become automatic (they're performed easily and quickly without thinking), so drivers can pay more attention to higher-level, strategic thinking. Project-based learning does not address this need to automate some lower-level skills.

4. Much learner time can be wasted during project-based learning by searching for information and struggling to learn without sufficient guidance or support.

Fortunately, the benefits of project-based learning can still be captured by providing appropriate instructional support during a project to address all four problems.

For example, technology already exists for creating a system whereby students in a team can work on an authentic project in a computer-based simulation, or virtual world, until they encounter a need to learn something new. At that point, project time might freeze and a virtual teacher would appear for each student, perhaps on her own personal work tablet, to provide individualized tutoring. The student could then work on developing the needed skill or acquiring the knowledge or attitude just in time for use in the project. This kind of tool is known as an *instructional overlay* for project-based learning. It can also be provided by a teacher instead of a computer-based tutorial or simulation, but using digital technologies for this assistance can greatly lower the cost of the assistance.

Research shows that people best learn a skill when they're told how to do it, shown how to do it, and can practice it with immediate feedback. Instructional overlay helps students learn to generalize or transfer a new skill to a range of cases he may encounter in the real world. The student continues to practice until he reaches the standard for competency—perhaps ten correct performances in a row, the metric used by the Khan Academy. Then he returns to the project to use it right away and continues working on the project until the next learning need is encountered, and this learning cycle repeats.

The instructional overlay has many benefits.

- It reduces frustration and learning time.
- It ensures that students can generalize learning to diverse situations.
- It allows for automating lower-level skills that need it.
- The mastery requirement ensures individual accountability in a team-based, holistic learning environment thus combining the best of constructivist learning and direct instruction approaches (another example of the "both–and" thinking that characterizes the Information Age).

Special Needs

The Information Age paradigm accommodates children with special needs in the very fabric of its design. In this paradigm, all children are special. Education is personalized for all children. All students are closely monitored for progress and receive the emotional and intellectual attention they require and deserve. Children with cognitive disabilities and other health- and medical-based problems are integrated fully into the education system and work on projects with all other types of children. Specialized staff are available when needed, as explained in "Core Idea 5: A Nurturing School Culture."

CORE IDEA 3: EXPANDED CURRICULUM

The goal of the Information Age paradigm is to develop people who

- are capable of creating a high quality of life for themselves, their families, and their communities;
- have the historical and civic knowledge to be good citizens of both their country and the global society; and
- can apply competencies that help them to succeed in their chosen careers.

These attributes apply to preparation for the workplace as well as to family life, civic responsibilities, and personal fulfillment. A fully functional education system must address all aspects of child development and provide students with the self-directed learning skills and motivation they need to continue their learning throughout their lives.

Pipe dream or possible? Before you answer, consider all the nonacademic things schools are already being asked to do. Yet educators can't even get all their students to perform at grade level in the basic subjects. Can we ask teachers to address all these other kinds of learning, too? Actually, not in the

Industrial Age paradigm, because its structure makes it almost impossible to meet student needs. But Information Age schools are already doing remarkably well with these additional kinds of learning and with learning in the academic subjects (see chapter 3).

At this point, you may be wondering what the important kinds of learning are.

National Reports

Recognizing that dramatic changes in the workplace have important implications for curriculum, the U.S. Department of Labor commissioned the Secretary's Commission on Achieving Necessary Skills (SCANs) Report for America 2000, which was released in 1991. In brief, that report recommended that primary and secondary school curriculum should include the following elements:

- basic skills, including the ability to read, write, perform mathematical operations, and listen and speak effectively
- thinking skills, including ability to think creatively, make decisions, solve problems, and visualize outcomes
- personal qualities, including responsibility, self-esteem, good interpersonal skills, self-management, and integrity
- competency in use of resources, information, technology, interpersonal skills, and systems thinking

Building on this foundation, in 2009 the Partnership for 21st Century Skills published its *Framework for 21st Century Learning*, which provided these updates to curriculum guidelines:

- Core subjects include English, reading or language arts, world languages, arts, mathematics, economics, science, geography, history, government and civics.
- 21st Century interdisciplinary themes, woven into core subjects, include global awareness; financial, economic, business, and entrepreneurial literacy; civic and health literacy.
- Learning and innovation skills include creativity, critical thinking, and problem solving, as well as communication and collaboration.
- Information, media, and technology skills include information literacy, media literacy, and communications literacy.
- Life and career skills cover flexibility and adaptability, initiative and self-direction, social and cross-cultural skills, productivity and accountability, and leadership and responsibility.

Other Kinds of Learning

A core of *character traits* and *democratic values* is important for the health of our democracy and our communities. Also, Daniel Goleman popularized the understanding that success in life depends more on one's *emotional development* (emotional quotient, or EQ) than intellectual development (intelligence quotient, or IQ).

Emotional development can save a lot of money for society (e.g., less crime and prison time) and improve the quality of life for individuals, communities, and nations. It has proven to reduce substance abuse, teen pregnancy, bullying, and other social problems. Poor emotional development also typically results in a "fight or flight" response that hurts learning, increases the odds of delinquency and imprisonment, and perpetuates a cycle of poverty.

On a larger scale, insufficient development of emotional intelligence and the core values of our democracy have arguably led to national and international problems, including the Enron scandal, the Madoff ponzi scheme, the global financial crisis of 2008, and many other incidents of corruption, violence, and crime. In fact, prison populations are predicted based on third-grade reading scores. It is far less expensive to educate children well than to incarcerate them.

The social and monetary costs of insufficient attention to emotional development and to nurturing core values in people are extremely high. In the Information Age paradigm of education, emotional and values development are addressed by the teacher throughout the day as teachable moments arise during students' interactions with each other, making the learning experience customized and authentic. These teachable moments are anticipated and valued as a part of the learning experience, rather than as distractions taking time away from what students should be learning. Such development occurs much more effectively in a classroom with teacher guidance than on the playground without it.

Finally, the importance of healthy *physical development* through exercise and nutrition is also increasingly evident.

The Information Age paradigm incorporates all the previously described curricular areas in its mission to foster all aspects of human development, including what Bela Banathy, a pioneer in systems thinking about education, refers to as the sociocultural, ethical, moral, physical/mental/spiritual wellness, economic, political, scientific/technological, and aesthetic dimensions of learning. Yet specific points of curriculum will need to adapt to advances in knowledge and changes in student needs and society's values.

The Information Age curriculum must provide students with a solid understanding of important concepts and principles and an ability to apply their understanding to real-life problems and situations. Many of the target areas of competency are the same for every student, but many others are different depending on an individual student's needs, talents, interests, and aspirations. Personal learning plans and customized teaching methods ensure that individual learning needs and styles are addressed.

CORE IDEA 4: NEW ROLES

Learner-centered instruction requires teachers, students, parents, and even technology and other learning resources to function dramatically differently from their roles in the Industrial Age system.

Teachers

In the Information Age paradigm, the teacher is not a judge who serves as a perceived threat to a student but is instead a guide or coach who helps students conquer obstacles. This is a move from teacher-centered to learner-centered education—from a teacher functioning as a sage on the stage to a guide on the side.

The teacher assumes these five roles in the Information Age education system:

1. *Mentor* for perhaps twenty to thirty students for several years, one who is concerned with all aspects of student development, as practiced in the Montessori system and the Minnesota New Country School (see chapter 3). It has been said, "Kids need to think that you care before they care what you think." Part of the mentor role is helping students prepare a personal learning plan for each project period, which runs for six to twelve weeks. This involves helping the student and parents choose appropriate instructional goals (subject to standards set by the community, state, and nation) and then helping to identify and support the best means for the student to achieve those goals.
2. *Designer* of student work options, mostly projects or tasks, to engage students in the learning process. Open educational resources that are developed by teachers throughout the country and available to all educators for free via the Internet can alleviate much of the burden of the designer role.
3. *Facilitator* of the learning process, which entails monitoring student progress, enhancing student motivation, and coaching student performance.
4. *Learner*, the teacher is always learning with the students, about the students, from and for the students. The teacher does not have all the

answers, but the teacher helps students find answers. And the teacher is always learning more about how best to meet students' needs. The Information Age paradigm provides sufficient support for teacher learning.

5. *Owner and manager* of the school. Like lawyers and accountants in a small firm, teachers are partners who own their public school and make decisions about its operations, including budgeting and staffing (see "Core Idea 6: Organizational Structures"), as the Minnesota New Country School is structured. This elevates the role of teachers to that of true professionals, rather than workers controlled by an all-powerful bureaucracy.

Some teachers specialize in one or two of these roles at which they excel. These roles for teachers are so different from their roles in the factory model of schools that some people argue that the term *teacher* miscommunicates the nature of this position in the Information Age system. Since the role is often characterized as that of a guide on the side, we use the term *guide* instead of teacher whenever talking about teachers in the Information Age paradigm.

Students

Students in the Information Age paradigm assume three new roles in place of the traditional role as isolated, passive learner.

1. *Self-directed learner.* Lifelong learning is critical for success in the Information Age, as discussed in chapter 1, and it requires self-directed learning, so students must be taught at an early age to manage their own learning process, as Montessori schools emphasize beginning at age three. Students need to learn to set goals and plan the means to achieve their goals. This includes figuring out how they learn best, what learning strategies and tools best serve their learning styles, and how to improve their learning styles. Learning to be self-directed requires some degree of student choice of both content and instructional methods, and guides help to cultivate students' ability to make good choices.

2. *Learner as teacher.* There is an adage that says the best way to learn something is to teach it. With that in mind, students may be the most underutilized resource in schools today. In the Information Age paradigm, students on a project team teach each other. And students who have already attained a competency standard tutor or coach other students who are still working to learn that material. Therefore, *student as teacher*

is another new role for students. This student role is already becoming more common in many schools.

3. *Collaborative learner.* In the "Collaborative Learning" section earlier in this chapter, we described a new role of students as collaborative learners, in contrast to the Industrial Age perspective that students are cheating if they collaborate. New methods are used in the new paradigm to ensure that students learn and don't cheat. Learning how to learn from and with peers will serve students well in all aspects of their lives, including their jobs and marriages.

Parents

Parents in the Information Age paradigm are more actively involved in deciding what their child will learn and helping her to learn it. Parents have access to specific guidance for fun things they can do with their child to help her learn—from questions to ask at different exhibits in the local zoo and information on what makes a good answer, to places to see and things to do on a vacation. Parents also have some input into how their child's school is run. Parents are true partners with their child's guide in the new paradigm.

Technology and Other Resources

Appropriate learning tools are vital to implementing the Information Age paradigm of education in a feasible and cost-effective way (see "Cost-Effectiveness" toward the end of this chapter).

To get a handle on the relationship between the tools of an age and the age itself, consider the role of the railroad in the Industrial Age. Manufacturing made the railroad necessary—to ship large quantities of raw materials and finished goods to and from factories. But it also made the railroad possible—because the railroad could only be created with industrial processes and tools.

Similarly, the Information Age makes the new paradigm of education not only necessary, but also possible, for it is greatly facilitated with digital technology. In fact, such technology has revolutionized all kinds of industries—from the electronic spreadsheet in accounting to imaging technologies in healthcare.

In the Information Age paradigm, digital technology and hands-on materials play a central role, as opposed to the small peripheral role they play in the current, teacher-centered paradigm. Digital technology is primarily for student use, rather than primarily for teacher use, in the new system.

Here, we describe the four main roles of technology in the Information Age. Note that we use the present tense to describe these roles, but we are not aware of any technology system that currently serves all these roles.

Recordkeeping for Student Learning

Keeping track of what every student has learned could be a nightmare for guides, especially when students are doing a lot of their learning in learning centers (away from the guide—see "Core Idea 6: Organizational Structures"). Technology is ideally suited to save guides huge amounts of time on monitoring records of student competency. The recordkeeping function of technology replaces the current report card and has three parts.

The *Record of Standards* includes both required educational standards (national, state, and local) and optional educational standards, broken down into individual competencies and arranged in learning pathways (when learning segments build on each other). Standards are easily accessed by guides, students, and parents. This technological tool presents a list or map of learning areas that the student should or can master, along with levels and criteria at which they can be learned.

The *Record of Personal Attainments* documents what each student knows. In essence, this record maps each student's progress on the standards listed in the Standards Inventory. It shows when a student met a standard, which standards were required, and what the next required standard is in each area. This record also provides links to evidence of competency (in the form of summary data and/or original products).

The *Record of Personal Characteristics* keeps track of each student's characteristics that influence learning, such as learning style, profile of multiple intelligences, student interests, and major life events.

Planning for Student Learning

Developing a personal learning plan, or contract, for all of their students could be difficult for guides. Fortunately, technology is ideally suited to fulfill this role in the Information Age paradigm. This role for technology helps each student, parent, and guide perform these tasks:

1. *Set long-term goals.*
2. *Consider options.* Identify the full range of attainments that are presently within reach for the student (based on the Record of Personal Attainments).
3. *Set short-term goals.* Select which options to pursue in the short term, based on requirements, long-term goals, interests, and opportunities.

4. *Select projects.* Choose from a menu of projects or design new projects as means for attaining the short-term goals.
5. *Assemble teams.* Identify other students who are interested in doing the same projects and select appropriate teammates.
6. *Assign roles.* Determine how the guide, parent, and other individuals might support the student in learning.
7. *Develop contracts.* A learning plan specifies goals, projects, teams, roles, and a timeline for each project.

Students in the Information Age education paradigm must learn to manage their time and meet deadlines, just like people do in the working world. But time available for various projects in the new system is flexible based on the number of projects each student takes on, and a student's workload during a given period is tailored to his abilities.

Instruction for Student Learning

Trying to teach twenty-five students who are all learning different things at any point in time would be very difficult if guides could only use Industrial Age, teacher-centered instruction. But that's not the case in the Information Age paradigm. Technology can introduce projects, provide instructional support during projects, help manage projects, and even help develop new projects and instructional support—all in a learning environment that fosters development of relationships among students and with guides.

Introduce Projects Technology (computers and mobile devices) can introduce a project to a student (or small team), often with simulations, virtual worlds, and engaging, interactive video. It can also provide project-management programs to help students succeed and project-tracking programs to help guides support student success.

Provide Instructional Support Technology can provide powerful instructional tools—simulations, tutorials, drill and practice, research tools, and communication tools—to support learning during a project and allow each student to spend as much time as needed in learning-by-doing (practicing) to attain each learning standard (much like the education program at the Khan Academy). This is basically an *instructional overlay* (described in "Core Idea 2: Learner-Centered Instruction") on project-based learning, and different kinds of instructional support are provided for development of specific attainments (such as higher-order thinking skills, deep understandings, memorization, emotional development) and different kinds of learners (based on their learning styles). While project work makes learning more fun, the instructional overlay makes the learning experience more effective and efficient and often reduces frustration.

Digital tools offer many benefits, including these:

- They're more dynamic in sight and sound than static resources and thus accommodate a greater variety of learning modalities.
- They offer powerful interaction for active student learning and immediate feedback.
- Internet access connects students and guides across geographic and cultural boundaries for a greatly enriched learning environment and eliminates the need to physically be in the same place at the same time.
- Staff development is available on demand—even in rural areas where teachers currently receive little support.
- These tools help guides monitor and support student progress on projects, and they help students monitor and reflect on their own progress and manage their time.

Yet high-tech resources are not the only technologies used in the Information Age paradigm; low-tech, hands-on resources, like number rods and sandpaper letters (see chapter 3), are also useful, especially for younger students. Learning resources are frequently designed for several students to use together, to promote learning with and from each other and to build strong relationships among students. Guides help students, through coaching and tutoring, as they use the resources, and they provide direct instructional support as necessary, complementing the high-tech and hands-on resources.

Help Manage Projects   Technology provides tools for monitoring and supporting student progress on a project, not just for guides, but also for students to monitor and reflect on their progress and manage their time.

Help Develop Instruction   Technology even provides tools to help guides and others develop new projects and new tools for the instructional overlay.

Guides and their assistants and volunteers assist students in their use of technology in their projects and instructional overlay, and they provide instructional support when technology cannot.

Assessment for and of Student Learning

Conducting formative and summative assessments of students could be a nightmare for guides in a world where students are demonstrating competency in different ways and at different times. Technology helps with these tasks.

In the instructional overlay—whether in a simulation or tutorial or drill and practice—the technology system is designed to provide formative feedback to the student and to evaluate whether the student meets the criteria for mastery of all the different kinds of learning.

When the criteria for successful performance have been met on, say, the last ten unaided performances, the summative assessment is complete and the corresponding attainment is automatically checked off in the student's Record of Personal Attainments. There is no separate assessment; the practice is the test, which saves a lot of time that would otherwise be wasted on testing. This is full integration of testing with instruction.

When interactive technology cannot assess a student's performance, an expert observer (perhaps using a handheld device with a rubric for assessment) evaluates performance and provides feedback. The information from the handheld device is automatically uploaded into the computer system, where it's placed in the student's Record of Personal Attainments.

Beyond student assessment, the computer system automatically analyzes the quality of the instructional tools, the guides, and the "schools" (which, by the way, are not called schools in the new paradigm because they are so different from what we know as schools today), and the information is used for both formative and summative purposes. Find more on how schools operate in the new paradigm in Core Ideas 5 and 6.

Finally, technology provides tools to help guides develop assessments and link them to the appropriate standards in the Record of Standards. These computer-generated assessment tools significantly reduce the amount of student and guide time currently devoted to carrying out assessment activities in the Industrial Age paradigm.

Integration of Tools

We envision that these four roles or functions of technology are seamlessly integrated, though such a system has yet to be developed as far as we know. We envision a system in which the recordkeeping tool informs the student-planning tool, which identifies instructional tools that are available to carry out the plans. Assessment processes are integrated into instructional tools and feed data to the recordkeeping tool. The student, parent, and guide all have easy access to progress reports on each of the student's projects and on the set of standards and individual attainments currently being pursued in the student's contract.

There is no label that describes this kind of comprehensive, integrated tool; recently, the term Personalized Integrated Educational System (PIES) was suggested. We like it!

In addition to the primary functions described earlier, we expect PIES to serve these and other secondary functions:

- communications, including e-mail, blogs, websites, discussion boards, wikis, whiteboards, instant messaging, podcasts, and videocasts

- administrative access to information and authority to input information based on role and information type
- documenting general student data, such as address, parent/guardian information, guide and cluster identification, student attendance, and medical information
- central resource on educator data, including office address, certifications and awards, professional development plan and records as well as a list of students (and their evaluations and earned awards) and repository of teaching tools they developed
- PIES will hopefully be open source software, similar to Moodle, making it affordable.

Ideally, it will be possible for districts, schools, and individuals to customize and modify the program for their own needs and to incorporate web apps (similar to iPhone apps) from various developers to support specific needs. Users can customize the look and function of their sites, controlling the flow of information into the site with RSS feeds and e-mail, and easily incorporating such features as blogs, discussion boards, and chats within PIES.

Indeed, technology plays a vital role in the success of the Information Age education paradigm. It enables a quantum improvement in student learning and likely at a lower cost per student per year than the Industrial Age paradigm (discussed in an upcoming section, "Cost-Effectiveness").

CORE IDEA 5: A NURTURING SCHOOL CULTURE

The Information Age education paradigm is characterized by a caring and supportive educational environment that features small school sizes, strong relationships, multiyear mentoring, multiage grouping into developmental levels, enjoyable learning, guides' learning, and family services. School culture has a profound effect on both students and guides.

Small School Size

Large schools tend to breed student alienation and the formation of adversarial cliques and bullying. They also require more administrative overhead than small schools, which provide a learning environment more conducive to caring and the development of emotional intelligence. However, among the advantages of large schools are:

- reduced costs for shared facilities, such as library, media center, cafeteria, gymnasium, and auditorium
- ability to offer a greater variety of courses

In the Information Age paradigm, the cost savings that large schools enjoy for shared facilities is resolved by placing shared facilities in a central area surrounded by small learning communities. Also, the greater variety of courses is neutralized by information technologies, open educational resources, and interactive multimedia programs over the Internet.

Strong Relationships

In addition to small cluster (school) size, each learning community in the new paradigm strives to form deep ties that connect students, guides, parents, and the larger community, often through collaborative projects and other relationship-building activities.

Multiyear Mentoring

Guide and students stay paired for a complete stage of child development (about three or four years), and each student has some choice of mentor for that time (see "Choice" in Core Idea 6). Getting to know each other well facilitates the growth of caring, trust, and support between a guide and student and provides a broader, more stable support network for the student.

Multiage Grouping into Developmental Levels

In all settings apart from schools, people associate with others of different ages. Younger people adopt older ones as role models, and older people assume some responsibility for younger people. In many situations, age isn't even a factor in social association. Instead, interests drive association. Similarly in the Information Age paradigm, a guide has roughly equal numbers of students across the age span for a developmental level.

The *first level* of development in the new paradigm begins at birth; all students get a head start! The learning at this level occurs either at home through parents and siblings (under guidance from a guide and/or a family services specialist as needed and desired by the parents), or with parents and a homeroom as a daycare option (with young assistants under the direction of a guide and/or family services specialist).

Family services include autism specialists and speech therapists. The guide and family services specialists provide advice and resources to parents as desired, to help them raise their children as well as they can. (More information is to follow about the family service organizations that are integrated into the new paradigm of education.)

The *second level* of development goes from about age three to six, when the children are concrete thinkers, as the Montessori system does (see chapter 3), and guides in the Information Age paradigm are similar to Montessori educators in many ways. That is, most of the learning occurs in a homeroom, where the guide and/or assistants introduce children to well-designed, hands-on resources as the children become ready for them to pursue specific types of learning. Caring educators have high expectations and nurture the full, well-rounded development of students in partnership with parents, to the extent desired by the parents. Guides also work to get parents more involved in their child's educational development, if necessary. The learning environment is designed to address children's drive toward order at this stage of their development.

The *third level* is very similar to the second except that the students—ages six to nine—assume more responsibility for planning and tracking their own learning. At this level, guides also help students transition from concrete to abstract thinking and work to hone their imaginations.

At the *fourth level*, ages nine to twelve, guides recognize that students have become abstract thinkers, and guides make connections between learning and the outside world through the nature of their projects and other means. Most of the students' work is done in the homeroom, but they begin going to learning centers (described next in Core Idea 6) and community sites (with supervision) for some of their learning.

The *fifth level* typically spans ages twelve to fifteen and is similar to Level 4 except that students do progressively more of their work at learning centers and community sites, so the homeroom has fewer resources and more meeting spaces and workspaces with digital technologies. Some schools use the mini economy—an experience-based instructional program designed to help students learn about economics, entrepreneurship, and government in a motivational way. It assists students in understanding the real world and can provide service to their communities.

At the *sixth level*, ages fifteen to eighteen, the facility is even more of a conference room with workspaces and little resemblance to the homeroom and activity room characteristic of lower levels. Most content learning occurs in learning centers (described in Core Idea 6), including center-sponsored seminars, projects, and tutoring sessions. Students tend to work in small groups. Project-based learning, including intellectual scavenger hunts entailing interdisciplinary problem solving, is widely used.

The guide also works with parents to develop the student's attitudes, values, and ethics; honesty, work ethic, responsibility, initiative, and perseverance are valued attributes for students in this paradigm. Students are required to complete community service projects, and the guide works closely with parents to address the child's emotional, social, creative, and psychological development. This entails identifying any aspects of development that warrant attention and obstacles to further development as well as developing an appropriate self-discipline plan with parents.

As child development levels, these categories do not entail rigid levels of skill or content learning. A child might be at a certain level based largely on her social and emotional development, but work on projects that are typically done by students in the next higher (or lower) level. In other words, "social promotion" is decoupled from "cognitive learning promotion." A nine-year-old could be studying college material without having to leave his peer group. Similarly, the child development levels do not represent rigid age levels because some children develop faster than others.

Enjoyable Learning

In the age of knowledge work and complexity, lifelong learning is essential to citizens' quality of life and the health of communities. Lifelong learning is greatly enhanced by love of learning. In the Industrial Age paradigm of education, many students hate learning, and the culture of schools devalues and derides students who excel in learning. That mindset and culture sabotage lifelong learning.

Although lifelong learning has, for many years, been a buzzword in education, the Industrial Age paradigm inherently impedes it. The Information Age paradigm, however, cultivates a love of learning in students by fostering intrinsic motivation, which requires learning though authentic, engaging projects or tasks. It also cultivates the skills for self-directed learning.

McClellan identifies three major human motives (intrinsic motivators), and the Information Age paradigm uses these motivators to inspire students to learn:

- The *need for achievement* is addressed by attainment-based student progress; a student checks off attainments as she meets standards.
- The *need for affiliation* is addressed by collaborative, team-based learning.
- The *need for power* is addressed by self-directed learning.

Guide Learning

One of the roles of guides in the Information Age paradigm is guide-as-learner (described in Core Idea 3). To be a good role model, the guide models lifelong learning. In the new paradigm, knowledge about content is far less important than knowledge about students and how they learn best. This learning is a journey that never ends, and it helps keep the teaching profession fresh and exciting for guides. The new paradigm places high priority on fostering all kinds of learning for guides, in part by having guides team with one or more other guides on the same developmental level. This allows them to learn from each other on a frequent basis.

Family Services

The school collaborates with social service agencies to provide various services to families, including development of parenting skills, advice about parenting, childcare support (on a cooperative basis, described in Core Idea 6), help with health and welfare issues, support for children's sports leagues, and so forth. The school system is an integrated part of a community development and services system.

CORE IDEA 6: ORGANIZATIONAL STRUCTURE AND INCENTIVES

The Industrial Age paradigm of education is dominated by top-down, bureaucratic decision-making structures, a focus on compliance (i.e., disempowerment of teachers and students), rigidity, seniority, political influence, and little-to-no choice for students or guides. In this section we describe an organizational structure that redefines schools. In the new paradigm we envision, organizational structures and decision-making systems include small guide-owned schools called *clusters*, learning centers, choice for students and guides, collaboration with family service support systems, and schools as "learning cooperatives."

Clusters as Schools

In the medical and legal professions, colleagues often consult with each other rather than working in isolation. Unlike teachers today, professionals in other walks of life participate in a meaningful way in decision making and have some control over the organizations in which they work. In a similar way, a guide in the Information Age paradigm does not work independently, but is a member of a cluster of guides who own and run their own cluster. This is a professional model of teaching rather than a supervisory (labor-management) model. This concept is so different from schools as we think of them today that the term *school* is a misleading term in the context of the new paradigm; we use the term *cluster*.

A cluster—containing four to ten guides, teaching assistants, and their students—functions somewhat like an independent contractor hired by the school district. In the larger Industrial Age school buildings, each cluster rents a separate wing or floor of the building and shares some facilities, such as the gym, library, and cafeteria. Anywhere from one to forty clusters are located in a single building, depending on its size.

New educational buildings have a very different design that places shared facilities in a central area, like the hub of a wheel, surrounded by a cluster on each spoke of the wheel.

In this setup, each guide has considerable responsibility for the success of the cluster and a high level of incentive and authority for meeting that responsibility.

Learning Centers

The guide and students have access to various learning centers as well as specialists and experts in other settings. A learning center provides instruction in a *focus area*, which might be any of the following:

- a traditional discipline-oriented area such as biology
- a cross-disciplinary thematic area such as pollution or cities
- an intellectual area such as philosophy
- a technical area such as automobile maintenance and repair

In all cases, centers integrate instruction on basic skills and higher-order thinking skills into the focus-area instruction, and the cluster guide helps each student put together a personal learning plan that represents a good progression for acquiring skills and meeting required standards.

At lower developmental levels, learning centers are seldom used, but a guide's homeroom contains mini learning centers, as in Montessori schools and the Minnesota New Country School (see chapter 3). At higher developmental levels, learning centers operate independently of clusters. Every few months students receive a certain number of passes that entitle them to use the learning centers; and students can earn additional passes.

The number of passes varies with developmental level, and clusters that issue fewer passes have more resource money to put into their own learning centers. Therefore, as a general rule, the older the child, the more she uses the centers.

Budgets for learning centers are based on the number of students served (the number of passes tallied), giving learning centers considerable incentive to attract students and satisfy cluster guides' needs. This means that a combination of competition among learning centers and cooperation within a center exists to maximize performance, again representing both–and thinking.

We envision three types of learning centers:

- *Shopping mall centers* are centrally located facilities ranging from a one-person "craft shop" operation to a regional or national chain. They offer powerful learning environments that incorporate a range of resources—from hands-on materials to web-based multimedia learning environments.
- *Community centers* are located in community settings, such as museums, zoos, and businesses. These centers bring in extra income and tax breaks for their sponsors to support the learning center activities, and they offer students important learning resources in real-world settings.
- *Mobile centers* travel from one cluster to another and even from one community to another. They are found mostly in low population areas and for particularly expensive learning resources, such as an electron microscope or a mass spectrometer.

As in retail businesses, competition pressures learning centers to adjust their offerings to meet the changing needs of students and their clusters. Learning centers spring up and die off on a regular basis. Incubation policies and resources encourage the formation of new learning centers to support a continuous renewal process. Cooperative arrangements are made so children may use learning centers located in other school districts such as the Challenger Learning Center in the Metropolitan School District of Decatur Township in Indianapolis. Learning centers are staffed by certified guides and technical and creative experts as well as parents and community members as volunteers.

Choice for Students and Parents

Students, or their parents, request, in order of preference, their choice of three to five guides. An independent Consumer Aid Agency (described under "Administrative Structures" next) provides information and assistance to parents to help them make the best decision or make it for them if they don't care.

Each guide decides how many children to accept each year but does not decide which children to accept; this policy ensures that students get equal access to a quality education. "Which children" is decided by a formula that maximizes the number of first choices filled district-wide, within the constraints of racial and socioeconomic balance guidelines. And each guide's pay varies in part according to the number of students she accepts. Also affecting pay is the cluster's success in teaching, which is measured by gains in all areas of learning and adjusted for factors such as students' learning capabilities and socioeconomic status.

If the number of first-, second-, and third-choice requests for all of its guides is high, a cluster gets a certain percentage increase in money for its guides' salary rates (regardless of how many students the guides accept), which provides an incentive for all guides to improve and for the best guides to remain in teaching. The Consumer Aid Agency helps to keep this request process from turning into a popularity contest by providing *Consumer Reports*–type ratings on all guides. Guides can choose to take a reduced load, or some may be forced to if they are in low demand. This mirrors the workload dynamic of other professions.

Competition among clusters can have negative effects unless the system is designed to avoid them. Therefore, the salary supplement for each *cluster* varies with the demand for its guides, not the salary supplement for each guide directly. The distribution of any salary supplement is determined collectively by the cluster guides, and a cluster's guides collectively decide how to spend their budget. This combines the benefits of competition among clusters (providing incentives for excellence and responsiveness to the community's diverse and changing desires and needs) and cooperation within each cluster (providing support and encouragement among guides).

Excluding the direct revenues for the guides' salaries, the revenue per child is equal across all clusters for a given developmental level, except for supplements for special-needs children and socioeconomic status. A cluster has full authority to decide how it spends that money, including the amount of space it rents from the school district, the amount of learning resources it buys or rents, and the number and type of support people it hires. In this regard, clusters are much like a charter school or private school.

A cluster whose guides are in high demand is able to accept more students, hire more support personnel, and even hire (or promote from within) new guides. On the other hand, a cluster with guides in low demand receives less salary money to split among its guides, and its guides receive less than a full salary if they don't have a full load of students. Therefore, a guide who is not successful receives less money and may decide to look for another job. In this way, personnel hiring and firing are separated from a bureaucracy-based decision-making process; these functions are replaced by an automatic client-based system that allows for constant adjustment to the changing needs of the community—and also lowers bureaucratic costs.

A rating mechanism allows other clients of education, such as employers and senior citizens, to provide input to the client-based decision-making system. This is done with a product rating system, similar to that used by Amazon, for rating individual guides or their clusters, which influences students' or parents' selection of guides.

Incubation policies encourage the formation of new clusters and learning centers. If a group of guides solicits enough parent signatures to support creation of a new cluster or learning center, the Cluster Support Agency or the Learning Center Support Agency assists in its creation with a grant for startup funds and expertise to plan and start operations. These agencies are described in greater detail later in the "Administrative Structures" section.

With several clusters in a single school building, parents and students have choice without needing to leave their neighborhood school. Further, students and parents have some choice about what to learn and how to learn as part of self-directed learning (described in "Core Idea 4: New Roles for Students").

Our current educational system is highly resistant to change, making a crisis necessary for significant change to occur. To avoid designing an Information Age system equally resistant to change, the new paradigm we envision is a self-adjusting learning organization. Crises are minimized because change is continuous and client-driven. Guides are in charge of adapting their practices to the changing educational needs of the community and students, rather than administrators and politicians controlling the changes.

Choice for Guides

Guides have choice about which cluster or learning center to apply to and, thus, to some degree, which other guides to work with. Of course, the guides in any given cluster or learning center have complete choice as to how many and which guides to hire. A guide can try to move to a different cluster at any time, and a guide can choose his developmental level and focus area. The new system removes these decisions from the bureaucracy-based decision-making process.

Administrative Structures

A district-wide administrative system facilitates the efforts of the clusters and learning centers. This system is designed to support rather than to control.

The Cluster Support Agency manages and supports the incubation of new clusters and may be contracted by existing clusters to provide support services to them—budget management, purchasing support, maintenance services, or transportation, for example. These services are outsourced to private contractors by the Cluster Support Agency at a group-negotiated rate.

The Learning Center Support Agency serves the same functions for the learning centers. Clusters and learning centers may opt out of these services and hire others better able to serve their needs. Both district-wide support agencies depend entirely on fee income from the clusters and learning centers for their budgets, except for the incubation services portion, which comes directly from the state; the agencies' income is based on the number of students they serve.

Alternatively, the Cluster Support Agency and the Learning Center Support Agency may be combined into a single agency to serve both clusters and learning centers, depending on the size of a particular school district.

The independent Consumer Aid Agency serves as a placement counseling service for matching children with guides. It provides diagnostic testing and interviews with students to help parents make the best decisions when choosing guides—and to actually make the choices for parents who don't want to participate in this process. This assistance can help to break the cycle of poverty by ensuring that all students are well matched with a guide.

This agency also serves as a watchdog service for collecting and disseminating information about the performance of clusters, guides, learning centers, and support agencies.

The PIES technology system (see "Core Idea 3: Technology and Other Resources") automatically analyzes the quality of its instructional tools. Measures of performance for each guide and cluster (in terms of student attainment of standards and other factors) are prepared by the agency and are available to parents and students. User ratings are also maintained to further help students and parents make good choices. Similar measures of each learning center's performance are prepared for cluster guides and students. Guides in the clusters and learning centers can also access this information so that they can make improvements.

The Consumer Aid Agency's budget comes directly from the state and is based on the number of students it serves, which keeps it independent and unbiased.

Governance Structures

On both the community and state levels of governance, the Information Age structure differs from the current Industrial Age system. Local district school boards set and monitor the attainment of community standards, and they oversee facilitation efforts of individual units (clusters, learning centers, and district support units). The district board also serves as a citizen review board that adjudicates disputes among stakeholders (guides, parents, students) and protects the rights of disadvantaged students. The district board does not micromanage the affairs of the educational system. The client-driven decision-making system provides local accountability in educational decisions.

Funding the district board may happen in several different ways. A fee or tax paid by all clusters based on revenues might be effective, or allocations from local property taxes might be the best option.

The state department of education in the Information Age paradigm sets statewide standards and monitors their attainment. The department no longer micromanages local systems or dictates how specific districts or schools achieve standards; instead the state department uses incentive systems and contingencies to correct deficiencies in standards attainment.

The department also functions as the money mover by managing an equitable revenue collection and distribution system. Money goes directly from the state to each cluster (bypassing the district board) through a formula based on the number of students, the age of each student, any special needs each student may have, and a supplement for socioeconomically disadvantaged students. A state-level review board is in place for cases that the district boards cannot resolve.

Property taxes are the most *regressive* way to support public education. In the current systems, lower-income people end up paying a larger proportion of their income to school taxes, and communities with fewer businesses are at a disadvantage. However, state income tax revenues fluctuate considerably from economic expansion to recession, and the periodic huge budget cutbacks have a strongly negative effect on schools.

One solution is to fund education with a dedicated portion of the state income tax, but this approach would require a reserve representing a certain percent of the annual education budget during years of economic expansion to be used to maintain the budget during years of reduced tax revenues.

Another solution is to use property taxes to fund education, but to set tax rates on a sliding scale, so less expensive single-family dwellings are charged a lower tax rate. However, this does not address the inequities inherent in some communities being poorer than others or having fewer businesses that pay school property taxes.

The new paradigm must find a revenue system that is both more stable throughout the economic cycle and more equitable across communities of differing means to support it.

Collaboration with Family Service Systems

Family services are more important than ever in modern society. Raising children is just more difficult in this age of complexity. Everything from installing a child car seat correctly and monitoring your child's use of the Internet to avoiding child predators and promoting good nutrition and exercise weighs heavily on many parents who also are typically working full time, volunteering with their children's activities, and trying to carve out a little time for themselves, friends, and each other.

With so many conflicting opinions, expectations, and studies out there, parents increasingly need a reliable source of information, someone to turn to with questions about parenting, health services, and much more. Social service agencies and schools need to collaborate more than ever before.

To meet the real needs of students in the Information Age, we think broadly of school systems as systems of learning and human development. This results in considerable overlap with traditional family service systems at both the community and state levels. Therefore, the new paradigm integrates services for newborns through five-year-old children and their families. The Independence (MO) School District has implemented such a collaboration for students and their families.

Family services include healthcare, parent education, counseling, childcare services for working parents, and family literacy efforts. In the new paradigm, most of these services are based in the cluster with caseworkers; healthcare workers provide some services in the school building and some at children's homes.

The school is the one place with which a majority of families associate for an extended period. The new paradigm maximizes the opportunities for leveraging that contact to shore up the family's resources and commitment to education and thus maximize the positive experience of children in schools.

A Learning Cooperative

The clusters and learning centers are a community learning hub that operates in partnership with the public library and functions as a learning destination for all members of the community. Individuals over the age of eighteen must earn credits to use the center by donating time to helping others learn, providing childcare services, volunteering in the cafeteria, providing custodial or maintenance services, or contributing to the operation of the clusters or learning centers in some other way.

Schools can thus be open to students from early in the morning to late at night, seven days a week, and the community's adults have flexible and affordable opportunities to advance their job skills, parenting skills, and other information needs, which strengthens communities.

Furthermore, community members support student learning in the community and in the clusters and learning centers. Students occasionally work with adult community mentors on projects involving service learning. To ensure this functions in a safe and reliable manner, all adults who provide such volunteer services to the school must pass appropriate background checks, and related liability insurance and legal issues must be addressed. But assuming that those logistics are handled appropriately, the learning cooperative concept goes far to lower the cost of public education and make it an effective educational system that truly serves the public.

Most of the core ideas of the Information Age education paradigm are supported by current research on human development and learning processes. Some of the ideas need revision; some are likely to vary at implementation from one community to another and even from one cluster to another within a community; and most need to be further operationalized. But we hope this vision provides a useful reference to help you jump out of the Industrial Age mindset about education and join the effort to reshape the U.S. educational paradigm into a working system that meets the real needs of students and communities living in the Information Age.

STRUCTURAL CHANGES

The six core ideas of the Information Age education paradigm have important implications for the structure of education systems. To examine these implications, first consider the structural features of the Industrial Age paradigm:

- grade levels
- class periods
- classrooms
- courses
- grades

It may seem hard to imagine a school system without these features, but none of them existed in the agrarian age paradigm of the one-room schoolhouse. They met important needs during the Industrial Age but are obsolete in the modern age. Further, these components of current education systems may actually be the source of problems with the current state of education.

- *Grade levels* are incompatible with the new paradigm because individual students learn at different rates and become ready to move on to different attainments at different times. Grade levels are a key feature of the time-based, sorting-focused paradigm that served us well during the Industrial Age, but they are detrimental to meeting Information Age educational needs.
- *Class periods* often cut learning short before a "learning episode" has had the opportunity to play itself out to a successful conclusion. Fixed time serves the sorting-focused paradigm well but is a detriment to the learning-focused paradigm.
- *Classrooms* are designed for a single teacher to work with a group of twenty-five or more students. For the new paradigm, spaces designed for

collaboration among guides as well as among students are imperative. Learning spaces must be full of rich resources (including technology) and project workspaces.

- *Courses* provide little flexibility for students to choose what to learn. It is more useful to think in terms of small units or modules of specific attainments and how to certify understanding.
- *Grades* function primarily to compare students to each other. Grades do not reveal what a student has learned. They are appropriate for a sorting-focused system but not for a learning-focused system genuinely committed to leaving no child behind.

Understanding that these structural features of the current paradigm are incompatible with the Information Age paradigm underscores the magnitude of the transformation required. Yet the six core ideas offer a sense of direction for the transformation, though the particulars of implementation may differ over time and from one school system to another.

Eventually, the education system that students need today and tomorrow will become clearer and gain momentum as it moves up its S-curve. Early versions of the new paradigm won't come close to reaching its potential, but they already outpace the current paradigm.

COST-EFFECTIVENESS

The Information Age paradigm offers greater effectiveness at lower cost than the factory model schools for these reasons:

- Attainment-based student progress enhances the effectiveness of the education system by avoiding huge wastes of time associated with holding back fast learners and the failures related to rushing slow learners and thereby ensuring that they accumulate gaps in their learning that make learning related material more difficult in the future.
- The increased motivation to learn that comes from project-based learning—when projects are strongly related to student interests—also improves the effectiveness of education efforts.
- Project-based learning that uses real-world projects results in better transfer of student skills to the real world.
- Eliminating layers of bureaucracy saves money, especially in larger, more bureaucratic school districts.
- Teaching support from aides and interns (beginning guides) allows lead guides on a developmental level to accept more students and still

provide students the personalized attention they need. This reduces costs per student.

- Self-directed learning, collaborative learning, and peer tutoring, all highly effective modes of learning, place fewer time demands on guides, so they can effectively serve more students, lowering the cost per student. Students are perhaps our most underutilized resource in education.
- The learning cooperative concept provides a way for parents, senior citizens, and other volunteers to play a much more meaningful role in helping students to learn. By encouraging volunteers to support the clusters and learning centers in exchange for access to the system's resources to further their own learning, adults in a community provide additional human contact while reducing labor costs and contributing to a greater sense of community.
- Increasingly cost-effective technology provides labor-saving instructional tools that allow guides to serve more students while still providing personalized learning and a caring learning environment.

Even if costs were not lower, the new paradigm is more effective at promoting student learning, so it would still be more cost-effective than the current paradigm.

Further, the social costs of inadequately preparing students for modern life include higher rates of crime, substance abuse, bullying, violence, and unethical behavior. The Information Age paradigm helps students build and maintain relationships, and develop social and emotional intelligence and strong ethical character; it also better prepares people for success in the workplace.

Chapter 3 describes how some schools are getting started with the Information Age paradigm, thereby showing how some different communities are implementing the six core ideas.

CHAPTER SUMMARY OF KEY IDEAS

- Core ideas for the new paradigm of education are based on the key characteristics and educational needs of the Information Age.
- These six core ideas for the Information Age education paradigm are described to stimulate thinking about what's possible for education, with the understanding that they may be implemented in many different ways in different communities.
- The six core ideas are summarized in table 2.1.
- Grades, grade levels, class periods, classrooms, and courses are all antithetical to the core ideas for the new paradigm.

Table 2.1. Core Ideas for the Learning-Focused Paradigm

Attainment-based system	Student progress	Each student must reach the standard before advancing and must be allowed to advance as soon as the standard is reached.
	Testing	Student assessment is both formative to assist learning and summative to certify individual mastery of each attainment. It does not produce grades, averages, or other student-to-student comparative measures.
	Student records	A record of attainments indicates what standards each student has attained (instead of grades), and each attainment may be linked to a portfolio item.
Learner-centered instruction	Personalized	Each student has a personal learning plan that customizes both content and methods to the individual's needs.
	Project-based	Students work on engaging, authentic projects that entail learning selected attainments.
	Collaborative	Students often work in small teams on the authentic projects.
	Individualized instructional support	Instructional support for project-based learning provides personalized tutorials for mastering skills just in time during the projects.
	Special needs	All children are special and fully integrated with the other children.
Expanded curriculum	SCANS	Basic skills Thinking skills and creativity Personal qualities Broad competencies
	Twenty-first-century skills	Core subjects Twenty-first-century interdisciplinary themes Learning and innovation skills Information, media and technology skills Life and career skills
	Holistic	All aspects of child development are addressed, including emotional, social, physical, and character as well as cognitive development.

(continued)

Table 2.1. *(Continued)*

New Roles	Teachers	Guides are caring mentors, designers (and/or selectors) of engaging student work, facilitators of student work, lifelong learners, and cluster owners.
	Students	Students are self-directed learners, teachers, and collaborative participants in learning.
	Parents	Parents are actively involved in both deciding what their child should learn and helping her learn it. Parents also have input into how the school operates.
	Technology and resources	Technology and hands-on resources play a central role to support planning, learning, assessment, recordkeeping, collaboration, and communication.
A nurturing school culture	Small school size	Small learning communities help develop student responsibility, caring, and leadership, and they improve quality of life for staff.
	Strong relationships	Deep personal ties connect students, guides, parents, and the larger community.
	Multiyear mentoring	Each student has a mentor guide for a developmental stage (about three years).
	Multiage grouping	A guide's students are evenly distributed across a developmental stage.
	Enjoyable learning	Intrinsic motivation is nurtured by learning through authentic, engaging projects that are relevant to the students' lives and interests.
	Guide learning	Guides model lifelong learning by learning with, from, about, and for students.
	Family services	The school collaborates with social service agencies to provide specialized services to families.
Organizational structures	Schools as clusters	About four to ten guides own their own small public school.
	Learning centers	Other guides own their own learning centers that students in all clusters can use to learn in different focus areas. Centers include "shopping-mall," community, and mobile centers.
	Choice for students and parents	Students and their parents have some choice of guide (and consequently cluster and school building) as well as some choice for what and how they learn. Demand for guides influences their pay. Bureaucracy is eliminated.

Choice for guides

Guides have some choice of which other guides to work with and how their school is run.

Administrative structures

A Cluster Support Agency and a Learning Center Support Agency support (don't control) the clusters and learning centers. A Consumer Aid Agency facilitates beneficial student and parent choices.

Governance structures

Local district boards set and monitor community standards, adjudicate disputes, and advocate for clusters and learning centers. State boards and education departments set and monitor state standards, support local districts, and manage finances.

Collaboration with other family service systems

The schools collaborate with many agencies to provide human services in school buildings.

A learning cooperative

The schools are a learning hub where all members of the community may go to learn in exchange for donating skills and services.

- The new paradigm is more cost-effective than the factory model of schools because it uses attainment-based student progress (which avoids a huge waste of student time), uses project-based learning (which improves student motivation and transfer), eliminates the bureaucracy, uses aides and interns, uses self-directed learning and peer tutoring or collaboration, uses the learning cooperative concept, uses more technological tools and materials, and creates important social cost savings.

NOTES

1. IEPs are used mainly in special education.
2. *Intrinsic motivation* refers to motivation that comes from inside the student, in contrast to *external motivation*, which comes from external factors such as grades, praise, or money.

RELATED READINGS

American Psychological Association Presidential Task Force on Psychology in Education. *Learner-Centered Psychological Principles: Guidelines for School Redesign and Reform*. Washington, DC: American Psychological Association and the Mid-Continent Regional Educational Laboratory, 1993.

Bransford, John D., Ann L. Brown, and Rodney R. Cocking, eds. *How People Learn*. Washington, DC: National Academy Press, 2000.

Covington, Martin V. "The Myth of Intensification." *Educational Researcher* 25, no. 8 (1996): 24–27.

Darling-Hammond, Linda. *Redesigning Schools: What Matters and What Works 10 Features of Good Small Schools*. Stanford, CA: School Redesign Network at Stanford University, 2002.

Egol, Morton. *The Education Revolution: Spectacular Learning at Lower Cost*. Tenafly, NJ: Wisdom Dynamics, 2003.

Gardner, Howard E. *Frames of Mind*. New York: Basic Books, 1983.

Goleman, Daniel. *Emotional Intelligence: Why It Can Matter More Than IQ*. New York: Bantam Books, 1995.

———. *Working with Emotional Intelligence*. New York: Bantam Books, 1998.

Jonassen, David. *Learning to Solve Problems: A Handbook for Designing Problem-Solving Learning Environments*. New York: Routledge, 2011.

Lewis, Catherine, Marilyn Watson, and Eric Schaps. "Recapturing Education's Full Mission: Educating for Social, Ethical, and Intellectual Development. In *Instructional-Design Theories and Models: A New Paradigm of Instructional Theory*, edited by Charles M. Reigeluth, Vol. II, 511–36. Mahwah, NJ: Lawrence Erlbaum Associates, 1999.

Lickona, Thomas. *Educating for Character*. New York: Bantam Books, 1991.

McClelland, David C. *The Achieving Society.* New York: Irvington Publishers, 1976.

McCombs, Barbara. "The Learner-Centered Model: From the Vision to the Future. In *Interdisciplinary Handbook of the Person-Centered Approach: Connections Beyond Psychotherapy*, edited by Jeffrey. H. D. Cornelius-White, Renate Motschnig-Pitrik, and Michael Lux. New York: Springer, 2013.

McCombs, Barbara, and Lynda Miller. *Learner-Centered Classroom Practices and Assessments: Maximizing Student Motivation, Learning, and Achievement.* Thousand Oaks, CA: Corwin Press, 2007.

McCombs, Barbara, and Jo S. Whisler. *The Learner-Centered Classroom and School: Strategies for Increasing Student Motivation and Achievement.* San Francisco: Jossey-Bass, 1997.

Miliband, David. "Choice and Voice in Personalised Learning." In *Schooling for Tomorrow: Personalising Education*, edited by OECD, 21–30. Paris: OECD Publishing, 2006.

Perkins, David N. *Smart Schools.* New York: Free Press, 1995.

———. *Making Learning Whole: How Seven Principles of Teaching Can Transform Education.* San Francisco: Jossey-Bass, 2010.

Reigeluth, Charles M. "The Search for Meaningful Reform: A Third-Wave Educational System." *Journal of Instructional Development* 10, no. 4 (1987): 3–14.

———, ed. *Instructional-Design Theories and Models: A New Paradigm of Instructional Theory.* Vol. 2. Mahwah, NJ: Lawrence Erlbaum Associates, 1999.

———. "Instructional Theory and Technology for a Post-Industrial World. In *Trends and Issues in Instructional Design and Technology,* 3rd ed., edited by Robert A. Reiser and John V. Dempsey, 75–83. Boston: Pearson Education, 2012.

Reigeluth, Charles M., and Robert J. Garfinkle. "Envisioning a New System of Education." In *Systemic Change in Education*, edited by Charles M. Reigeluth and Robert J. Garfinkle, 59–70. Englewood Cliffs, NJ: Educational Technology Publications, 1994.

Reigeluth, Charles M., Sunnie L. Watson, William R. Watson, Pratima Dutta, Zengguan Chen, and Nathan Powell. "Roles for Technology in the Information-Age Paradigm of Education: Learning Management Systems." *Educational Technology* 48, no. 6 (2009): 32–39.

Savery, John R. "Problem-Based Approach to Instruction." In *Instructional-Design Theories and Models: Building a Common Knowledge Base*, edited by Charles M. Reigeluth and Alison A. Carr-Chellman, 143–65. New York: Routledge, 2009.

Schlechty, Phillip C. *Working on the Work.* New York: Wiley, 2002.

Schwartz, Daniel L., Xiaodong Lin, Sean Brophy, and J. D. Bransford. "Toward the Development of Flexibly Adaptive Instructional Designs." In *Instructional-Design Theories and Models: A New Paradigm of Instructional Theory*, edited by Charles M. Reigeluth, Vol. II, 183–213. Mahwah, NJ: Lawrence Erlbaum Associates, 1999.

Sturgis, Chris, and Susan Patrick. "When Success Is the Only Option: Designing Competency-Based Pathways for Next Generation Learning." Vienna, VA: International Association for K–12 Online Learning, 2010. Available at www.inacol.org/research/docs/iNACOL_SuccessOnlyOptn.pdf.

Wagner, Tony. *Making the Grade: Reinventing America's Schools*. New York: Rout-
ledgeFalmer, 2002.
Weimer, Maryellen. *Learner-Centered Teaching: Five Key Changes to Practice*. San
Francisco: Jossey-Bass, 2002.
Wolf, Mary Ann. "Innovate to Educate: System [Re]Design for Personalized Learn-
ing." Washington, DC: Software and Information Industry Association, 2010.
Yonezawa, Susan, Larry McClure, and Makeba Jones. "Personalization in Schools."
In *Students at the center series*. Quincy, MA: Nellie Mae Education Founda-
tion, April 2012. Available at www.nmefoundation.org/research/personalization/
personalization-in-schools.

RELATED WEBSITES

EDUCAUSE: www.educause.edu

The Khan Academy: www.khanacademy.org

The KnowledgeWorks Foundation: http://knowledgeworks.org

The National School Boards Association's Center for Public Education: www
.centerforpubliceducation.org

The Nellie Mae Education Foundation: www.nmefoundation.org

The New Commission on the Skills of the American Workforce: www
.skillscommission.org

Next Generation Learning Challenges: http://nextgenlearning.org

The Partnership for 21st Century Skills: www.21stcenturyskills.org/

The Secretary's Commission on Achieving Necessary Skills: wdr.doleta.gov/
SCANS/whatwork/

The Software and Information Industry Association: www.siia.net

The Virginia Council on Economic Education: www.vcee.org/programs-awards/
view/3

3

Examples of the New Paradigm

The attainment-based paradigm that we envision for the Information Age is not new. It has been around in various forms for well over a century, thanks to visionary thinkers like Maria Montessori and John Dewey—as well as the Boy Scouts. But because this education paradigm is incompatible with an industrial age society and Industrial Age thinking, it has not yet become the predominant paradigm for education in the United States.

In this chapter we point out how the six core ideas in the Information Age education paradigm described in chapter 2 are being used by three kinds of school systems:

- an individual school, the Minnesota New Country School
- a school district, the Chugach School District
- a broad network of schools, the Montessori system

For each of these three case studies, we provide general information about the school system, evidence of the implemented features' effectiveness, a table showing the extent to which each of the six core ideas is evident, and a description of how the core ideas are implemented in the system.

An at-a-glance table comparing these three school systems is presented in appendix A.

MINNESOTA NEW COUNTRY SCHOOL (EDVISIONS)

The Minnesota New Country School (MNCS) is a public charter school located in Henderson, Minnesota. It was founded in 1994 and has about 110

63

students in grades sixth through twelfth. Due to its success (described next), the MNCS received a $4 million replication grant from the Bill and Melinda Gates Foundation, with which they formed EdVisions, a not-for-profit organization dedicated to helping other schools to adopt the MNCS model. EdVisions has now helped more than forty schools to adopt the MNCS model, which is described in this case study.

Evidence of Effectiveness

MNCS reports the following effectiveness metrics in its 2010–2011 Annual Report:

- The ACT average composite score for all graduates from MNCS in 2007–2008 was 25.7 (the national average was 20.9).
- The ACT average composite score for all graduates from MNCS in 2010–2011 was 25.0 (the national average was 21.1).

EdVisions reports the following performance metrics on its website:

- The ACT average composite score for students from EdVisions Schools in 2007–2008 was 22.3 (the national average was 21.0).
- The SAT average composite score for students from EdVisions schools in 2007–2008 was 1749 (the national average was 1518).
- More than 82 percent of EdVisions graduates went on to two- or four-year degree programs in 2008 (the national average is 68 percent).
- Alumni from MNCS, the flagship EdVisions school, report 69 percent are graduates of two- or four-year degree programs, and 22 percent are still enrolled—a total of 91 percent!
- Of MNCS alumni, 92 percent report they felt better prepared for college than their peers.
- Eighty-three percent of graduates of EdVisions schools in Minnesota felt competent in working toward their goals.
- Of MNCS alumni in the workforce, 72 percent said about their jobs that they either "like it a lot," or "love it."

EdVisions also offers nontraditional measures worth noting. For life skills, an alumni survey of MNCS graduates reported percentages of alumni who graded the school as good or excellent in instilling the skills shown in table 3.1.

Core Ideas

Table 3.2 shows our rough estimation of how thoroughly MNCS has implemented the core ideas described in chapter 2. A six-point rating is used;

Table 3.1. Alumni Ratings of Skills Learned at MNCS

Skills Learned at MNCS	Percent of Alumni Grading MNCS as Good or Excellent
Creativity	100%
Problem solving	95%
Decision making	91%
Time management	87%
Finding information	100%
Learning to learn	91%
Responsibility	92%
Self esteem	84%
Social skills	79%
Self-direction	92%
Leadership	84%

Table 3.2. Core Ideas in the MNCS

1. Attainment-based system	Attainment-based student progress	5
	Attainment-based assessment and certifications	5
	Attainment-based student records	5
2. Learner-centered instruction	Customized (personalized) learning	5
	Project-based (task-based) learning	5
	Collaborative learning	3
	Individualized instructional support	5
3. Expanded Curriculum	SCANS curriculum	4
	21st-century skills	4
	All aspects of development	5
4. New Roles	for teachers (guides)	5
	for students	5
	for parents	4
	for technology	3
5. A nurturing school culture	Small school size	5
	Strong relationships	5
	Multiyear mentoring	5
	Multiage grouping	5
	Enjoyable learning	5
	Learning by guides	3
	Family services	0
6. Organizational structures	Schools as clusters	5
	Learning centers	3
	Choice for students	5
	Choice for guides	5
	Administrative structures	NA
	Governance structures	NA
	Ties to other family service systems	4
	A learning cooperative	0

Note: The number indicates the strength of the core idea, with five representing excellent implementation of the idea.

"zero" indicates that the core idea is apparently not used in the school, and "five" indicates that the idea is, in our opinion, exhibiting an excellent level of application. The table is followed by a description of the core ideas as implemented in the MNCS. More information is available about MNCS and EdVisions at these websites:

www.newcountryschool.com/
www.edvisions.com/custom/SplashPage.asp
www.whatkidscando.org/archives/portfoliosmallschools/MNCS.html

Core Idea 1: Attainment-Based System

Students' progress in this school is based on successful completion of projects. After students complete a project, they must present and defend the project before a panel consisting of a parent, the student's advisor, and two other advisors (what we call guides in this book)—the same panel that approved the proposal for the project.

Each student develops his own detailed, self-assessment rubric for each project. The rubric includes three main categories: project skills (e.g., task completion), critical-thinking skills, and performance skills (e.g., organization). Instead of a grade, the student receives credits for her project work. The panel decides how many credits the student will receive, based on demonstrated achievement through authentic assessment.

A student graduates from high school when he has completed all of the requisite state standards as well as seventy project credits, required life skills, and a senior project.

Core Idea 2: Learner-Centered Instruction

Students create their own academic programs through self-directed, individualized, and occasionally small-group learning projects. Each student works with an advisor to complete a project proposal form that specifies what she will do, the resources she will use, a timeline for completing project tasks, what state standards will be met, and how much credit she seeks for doing the project. The proposal must be approved by a panel (the same one that evaluates the project when it's complete) before the student may initiate work on the project. The approved proposal serves as a learning contract.

This process allows each student to explore topics that interest her in her own way and largely at her own pace. She then works with different advisors at the school (and often with other students) and experts from the local community or professors at the local university to carry out her projects.

The school offers "on-demand" seminars and "how-to" workshops to provide direct instruction and practice in support of student projects. Basic skills instruction is provided to individuals or small groups when diagnostic assessments reveal the need. Students engage in experiential activities, such as service-learning, place-based learning, internships, and even community college courses.

Children with cognitive disabilities have the same self-directed, project-based learning experiences as all other children. Rather than mainstreaming special needs children into a standardized classroom, the opposite happens here; all students receive personalized learning with individual learning plans.

Core Idea 3: Expanded Curriculum

Recently, MNCS established expectations for three areas: respect/responsibility, academic achievement, and engagement. Each area has four levels of development, and a student's privileges increase with each level. For example, regarding responsibility, level-one students have supervised computer and Internet use, whereas level-four students use their personal computers with Internet access and e-mail any time.

In addition to these three core areas, social, emotional, and other aspects of development are fostered through group projects, peacekeeping circles, life skills, a Restorative Justice program, and other means (described in the MNCS *2011–12 Annual Report*).

Academic achievement is driven by Minnesota state standards, but students design their own interdisciplinary projects to meet those standards. There are clear expectations and rules, including the expected pace of ten credits per year and seventy credits by graduation. A credit is roughly one hundred hours of work, but that is adjusted based on the quality of the student's effort, making it less of a time-based criterion and more of an attainment-based one. Each student is also required to spend one hour each day on math and have a daily quiet reading period.

Core Idea 4: New Roles

Teachers are called *advisors* in the MNCS, and they serve two major roles: teaching and administration.

For the teaching role, the advisor is a facilitator of learning rather than a disseminator of knowledge. This means that advisors do not define the course sequence for students; they do not set the syllabus for each course; and they don't pick texts for student reading, assign work, create deadlines, measure progress, or give grades. In fact, there aren't any courses as we know them in the current U.S. educational system. Instead, students have control over these matters, with advisor guidance as described in the previous section, "Core Idea 2: Learner-Centered Instruction." Each advisor serves a generalist role as a mentor for a group of fifteen to eighteen students, called an *advisory*, but also serves a specialist role for a particular subject area or two.

For the administration role, the advisors collectively run the school without a principal (find more on this in Core Idea 6).

Students are self-directed learners, and advisors contact parents fairly regularly by phone or e-mail to encourage them to engage significantly in their students' learning. Students have a democratic role in the operation of the school through a weekly town meeting and a student senate made up of two elected representatives from each advisory group.

MNCS is a high-tech learning environment in which all students have their own personal computer with Internet access, and responsible ones have unrestricted access to the Internet.

In 2005 the school adopted Project Foundry, an electronic standards tracking and reporting system, to help students manage their projects and learning progress and to help staff monitor and support student progress. It also supports electronic student portfolios. Thus technology plays an increasingly central role in MNCS and is used mostly for managing projects and accessing resources. It is not used much for direct instruction. Students are encouraged to learn from each other.

Core Idea 5: A Nurturing School Culture

The school is small; the student body totals about 110 pupils. Great effort is placed on building relationships among students, advisors, and people in the community. To this end, individualized computer-based instruction is minimized. The advisory groups are mixed-age and can include all age levels. There is no division into developmental levels. Each advisor gets to know his students very well and builds caring relationships. Family services are minimal. Great emphasis is placed on intrinsic motivation and self-directed learning.

Core Idea 6: Organizational Structures and Incentives

MNCS is a small professional organization centered on learning; EdVisions keeps its schools under 150 students. Advisors own and run the school without a principal and without supervisory control by a school district office. Therefore, it fits the definition of a cluster as described in chapter 2.

MNCS has a 17,000-square-foot room called the Atrium in which all students spend most of their time, much like the one-room schoolhouse that characterized education in the Agrarian Age. The building also has small rooms that serve as specialized learning centers including,

- a science room where students conduct experiments
- an arts studio with a pottery wheel and kiln, a recording studio, and materials for making stained glass and screen-printing t-shirts
- a greenhouse
- a wood shop
- a mechanics/metal shop
- a media center

All students who attend the MNCS made a choice to go to this public charter school. Also, at the beginning of the school year, students rank order the advisors that they want to work with, and they are usually assigned to one of their top choices. The advisors' jobs depend on the school attracting enough students. This provides great incentive for the advisors to meet their students' needs and listen to their students' parents. This is a *client-driven* element of the decision-making system. However, because the advisors make all the administrative decisions by consensus, there is also a *peer-based* decision-making element. Additional incentives for advisors come from performance-based pay, which is influenced by evaluations from peers, students, and parents.

The school calendar is designed to facilitate organizational learning. Normal operations take place throughout the year in five- to seven-week blocks. Following each block, advisors have a planning week that allows them time to talk and think about their approach to guiding student work. Peers, students, and parents complete advisor evaluations, which provide valuable information for advisor and organizational learning.

There is no principal. The school is run, both instructionally and administratively, by a cooperative of advisors using a consensus model. The advisor cooperative has a contract with the school board to provide administrative and other services. Each advisor serves on at least two of the seven management committees that make all the decisions about instruction and administration in their school (including budget and staffing), within the limits of the law.

The school is governed by an eight-member school board elected annually. It currently has four staff members, three parents, and one community member (see figure 3.1). A finance committee handles the finances and signs checks. A single-purpose authorizer, Novations Education Opportunities, is now the authorizer (previously the local school district was the authorizer). The authorizer provides oversight to ensure that the school meets academic, budgetary, and administrative standards.

Chapter 3

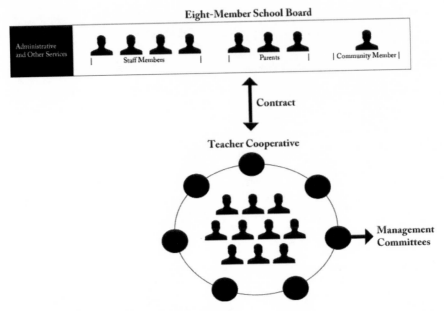

Figure 3.1. Organizational Chart for MNCS

The MNCS contracts various providers but does not yet have a cooperative relationship with any. The school contracts the RiverBend Education District to be its Special Education Director and receives services that include a school psychologist working on site one day per week and specialists available as needed to address autism, hearing, speech, and transition (moving students with disabilities into life after high school) needs. MNCS also contracts Sibley County Public Health to provide a nurse one day per week. It will contract with other agencies as need arises.

Cost-Effectiveness

The MNCS has a lower cost per student than the average school in Minnesota. Among other initiatives that save funds, the students clean the school every day, giving them more of a sense of ownership and pride, as well as money for educational resources.

RELATED READINGS

Aslan, Sinem. "Investigating 'The Coolest School in America': A Study of a Learner-Centered School and Educational Technology in the Information Age." PhD dis., Indiana University, 2012.

Dirkswager, Edward J., ed. *Teachers as Owners: A Key to Revitalizing Public Education*. Lanham, MD: Scarecrow Press, 2002.

Minnesota New Country School. *2011–12 Annual Report*. Available at www .newcountryschool.com/wp-content/uploads/2012/04/Annual-Report-2011-12.pdf

Newell, Ronald J. *Passion for Learning: How Project-Based Learning Meets the Needs of 21st-Century Students*. Lanham, MD: Scarecrow Press, 2003.

Thomas, Doug, Walter Enloe, and Ron J. Newell, eds. *"The Coolest School in America": How Small Learning Communities Are Changing Everything*. Lanham, MD: Scarecrow Press, 2005.

THE CHUGACH SCHOOL DISTRICT

The Chugach School District (CSD), with offices based in Anchorage, Alaska, has about 300 students scattered throughout 22,000 square miles of mostly isolated areas of South Central Alaska. Given its geographical circumstances and the demographics of its student body, CSD necessarily operates as a customized rather than standardized education system.

More than half of the students are homeschooled with district support; the others attend one of three schools in different communities. CSD delivers instruction from preschool up to age twenty-one in a comprehensive, attainment-based system.

CSD today is the result of a paradigm change effort that was initiated in 1994 by Roger Sampson. Education at CSD occurs twenty-four hours a day, seven days a week. Instruction is delivered in the workplace, the community, the home, and in school. Half of the students in the Chugach School District are Alaska natives.

Evidence of Effectiveness

According to the Consortium for School Networking (CoSN) Initiative, "Results have been dramatic on the California Achievement Test: reading scores rose from the 28th percentile in 1995 to the 71st in 1999; math scores increased from 54th to 78th; and in language arts from 26th to 72nd. Fourteen of 17 CSD graduates since 1994 are attending post-secondary institutions [compared to only a few in the previous 20 years]. . . . Faculty turnover has dropped from over 50 percent to 12 percent."[1]

In 2001, the CSD won a Malcolm Baldrige National Quality Award (which recognizes performance excellence) and became the smallest organization to win this award and one of the first educational institutions to win. It is also the only school district in the United States to be awarded the New American High School Award, a national award for top performing high schools.[2]

Wendy Battino, Rick Schreiber, and Rich De Lorenzo formed the Re-Inventing Schools Coalition (RISC) in 2002 to help other school districts adopt the CSD model (www.reinventingschools.org), but there are no formal relations between CSD and RISC.

Core Ideas

Table 3.3 shows our rough estimation of how thoroughly Chugach is implementing the core ideas described in chapter 2. A description of the core ideas

Table 3.3. Core Ideas in the Chugach School District

1. Attainment-based system	Attainment-based student progress	5
	Attainment-based assessment and certifications	5
	Attainment-based student records	5
2. Learner-centered instruction	Customized (personalized) learning	5
	Project-based (task-based) learning	4
	Collaborative learning	4
	Individualized instructional support	4
3. Expanded Curriculum	SCANS curriculum	3
	21st-century skills	4
	All aspects of development	4
4. New Roles	for teachers (guides)	5
	for students	5
	for parents	1
	for technology	4
5. A nurturing school culture	Small school size	5
	Strong relationships	4
	Multiyear mentoring	5
	Multiage grouping	5
	Enjoyable learning	3
	Learning by guides	5
	Family services	0
6. Organizational structures	Schools as clusters	3
	Learning centers	2
	Choice for students	3
	Choice for guides	3
	Administrative structures	2
	Governance structures	2
	Ties to other family service systems	4
	A learning cooperative	0

Note: The number indicates the strength of the core idea, with five as highest.

as implemented in Chugach follows. More information about the school district is available at:

www.chugachschools.com/
www.edutopia.org/chugach-school-district-reform
3d2know.cosn.org/best_practices/chugach.html
www.nwrel.org/nwedu/09-02/chugach.asp

Core Idea 1: Attainment-Based System

Each student in the Chugach school district has a Student Learning Profile, which outlines current attainment levels (as well as learning styles, strengths, and weaknesses as described in the section, "Core Idea 2"). This profile is used to inform the student, teacher, and parents about student progress.

Every secondary school student knows which level she is at. For example, she might be at level five in math, level seven in reading, level six in career development, and so forth. To move to the next level, she must master the one that precedes it.

Instead of grades, each student receives one of four ratings for each standard:

• emerging
• developing
• proficient
• advanced

The ratings are determined in different ways, including observation, projects, written work, performances, tests, and portfolios. Every student must learn every subject at every level, passing with a "proficient" rating. Each student has an electronic equivalent of what was initially an Assessment Binder that contains information (both formal and informal) aligned to the standards. Also, every student has a Student Lifeskills Portfolio, which supports and documents her progress toward proficiency in all standards.

Core Idea 2: Learner-Centered Instruction

Each Student Learning Profile portrays the student's learning styles, strengths, and weaknesses as well as the student's progress. Teachers and students use the Profile to customize instruction by providing input into the student's Individual Learning Plan, which uses a goal-setting and action-planning process with deadlines and accountability measures. The learning goals and accountability measures are set by the student.

Students complete some of the district standards through projects, which typically have real-world relevance, such as research on the local effects of climate change. Students and teachers work together to identify needs and interests of the student, school, and community to define projects that will have relevance and meaning to their lives. Then the instruction, direct and application-based, is designed around the project to help the student gain the necessary skills to be successful. Textbooks and some other learning materials also make up parts of the instructional support. These are all tied to each student's individual standards to meet their learning objectives.

All children are viewed as having special needs to some extent. Learning experiences are tailored to the needs of each student.

Core Idea 3: Expanded Curriculum

The CSD has more than 1,000 learning standards that span from kindergarten to high school graduation. The standards fall into ten areas, including the five conventional areas of math, reading, writing, science, and social studies as well as personal, social, PE/health, service learning, career development, technology, communication and culture (particularly about Alutiiq culture, the main culture of the Alaskan natives in the area). Thus, the curriculum addresses the whole child; the education system considers all aspects of a child's development.

The standards are broken down to the individual skill level. For example, reading comprehension is separated into standards such as isolating the initial sounds in words and retelling a story from memory. Standards are arranged on a continuum of levels, each of which must be mastered before the student moves on to the next level (but of course the standards are often mastered in interdisciplinary projects). Thus, CSD graduation requirements exceed state requirements in two major ways. First, all students must reach true proficiency in all standards. Second, the ten content areas require a broader array of standards than does the state. Teachers often integrate several standards into larger thematic units that span content areas and levels.

Core Idea 4: New Roles

Teachers collaborate with students to design projects, and they support students in conducting their projects. They also provide direct instruction when needed. These are both elements of Core Idea 2: Learner-Centered Instruction.

Students' roles center on taking ownership of their education. They complete their education at a pace that follows their proficiencies, graduating anywhere from age fourteen to twenty-one. As students get older, they assume more responsibility for their own learning. Students commonly work collaboratively in groups on projects while being assessed on their individual learning goals.

Regarding technology, in 2002 CSD adopted an electronic system to help teachers monitor each student's progress in the Student Learning Profile without drowning in paperwork. This system has evolved into a rich database of information that has many analytical tools that help the teachers identify learning styles and social/emotional quotients and assess achievement and ability. These help both teachers and students make instructional decisions, such as what standards to master next and what kinds of instructional support will be most effective.

Technology also plays an integral role in learning and instruction. Students who achieve proficiency at level four on all ten district content areas are eligible for a laptop provided by the district. In addition, each school has desktop computers in classrooms and an iPad lab. Between laptops and iPads, a one-to-one ratio of computers to students exists in each school. Each teacher is also provided a laptop by the district.

Core Idea 5: A Nurturing School Culture

CSD has three small schools, and students and teachers have strong relationships, founded on caring, trust, and respect. Students are no longer assigned to grade levels, and they keep the same teacher for several years. Students of different ages are grouped together and receive instruction based on their developmental levels. Learning is made enjoyable by having students participate in defining their own projects to meet the standards.

Teachers have incentives and support to work together, which encourages them to learn together. For example, collaborative support and mentoring are promoted through professional learning communities and team teaching, with veteran teachers coaching new teachers. And all Chugach teachers receive an *identical* annual performance bonus (sometimes exceeding $10,000) based on the average of their evaluations. This means teachers get a higher bonus if they help their fellow teachers improve. So teachers spend more time together learning techniques and developing skills. Teacher learning is also supported by thirty days each year that are set aside for staff development.

Core Idea 6: Organizational Structures and Incentives

Roughly two-thirds of the 300 students in the 22,000 square miles of CSD attend physical school sites; the other 100 students are in homeschool/

extension. With about 200 students attending the three schools, the learning environment is warm and caring. Students do not have choice of schools or of teachers, but they do have choice about what they study and when they study, based on their Individual Learning Plan (see the previous section on Core Idea 2).

Teachers also seem to have considerable autonomy within their role (see the previous section on Core Idea 4). Instructional decisions are primarily made at the school level by teachers, students, and community members. Central office staff play a supportive role.

Due to the small number of students in such a large geographical area, this district has no learning centers.

There is a single principal for the three schools in the district. At each school a head teacher handles the day-to-day administration of the school with the support of the district principal. CSD's school board is elected by the communities in the district. The school board provides overall policy guidance and oversight, a role similar to most other elected boards.

CSD collaborates with local service organizations, including those providing health and safety services. To some extent, the schools serve as community centers.

Cost-Effectiveness

Chugach supplements its $5,380 per-pupil allocation with about $1 million per year in grants, but the standards-based model does not require extra funding. In fact, the roughly ten-to-one student-teacher ratio is the result of having only about 300 students scattered over 22,000 square miles, rather than a requirement of this paradigm of education. Having more students in each school would allow more collaboration among students who are on the same level, more learning from peers, more efficiency for the facilitation role of teachers, and much lower travel expenses.

RELATED READINGS

Battino, Wendy. "New Horizons for Learning." Chugach School District. March 2002. Accessed May 17, 2010. www.newhorizons.org/trans/battino.htm.

CoSN. "Chugach School District: Rural Response to Local Expectations." A *Best Practices Case Study* by the Consortium for School Networking (CoSN) Initiative. Accessed February 5, 2013. www.cosn.org/Initiatives/3DDataDrivenDecision Making/CaseStudies/3D CaseStudyChugachSchoolDistrict/tabid/5701/Default.aspx

DeLorenzo, Richard A., Wendy J. Battino, Rick M. Schreiber, and Barbara G. Carrio. *Delivering on the Promise: The Education Revolution.* Bloomington, IN: Solution Tree, 2009.

Rubenstein, Grace. "Northern Lights: These Schools Literally Leave No Child Behind." *Edutopia.* (September 2007). www.edutopia.org/chugach-school-district-reform

Related Websites

Malcolm Baldridge National Quality Award, Education Criteria for Performance Excellence: www.nist.gov/baldrige/publications/upload/2011_2012_Education_Criteria.pdf
The Re-Inventing Schools Coalition (RISC): www.reinventingschools.org

THE MONTESSORI SYSTEM

One of the earliest examples of the Information Age paradigm is the Montessori system, which was developed by Maria Montessori around 1910, long before the beginning of the Information Age. Montessori is a true learner-centered approach to education that was designed with a deep and genuine respect for children as unique individuals.

At least 4,000 certified Montessori schools are operating in the United States, and about 7,000 exist globally. About 200 public schools in the United States and Canada offer certified Montessori programs. This is a very large and popular international school model.

Evidence of Effectiveness

In 2006 the journal *Science* published a study on students (at ages five and twelve) in public, inner-city Montessori schools, comparing them to control students who had lost a lottery to attend the Montessori school and therefore went to a variety of conventional schools instead. The study concluded that the Montessori students performed better than the students who went to other schools. This higher performance was achieved not only in traditional academic areas such as language and math but also in social skills.[3]

At the end of kindergarten, the Montessori children performed better than the other children on standardized reading and math tests, engaged in positive interaction on the playground more frequently, and showed more advanced social skills and self-control. The Montessori students also showed more concern for fairness and justice. At the end of elementary school, the Montessori children wrote more creative essays, used more complex sentence structures, chose more positive responses to social dilemmas, and felt more of a sense of community at their school.

These findings are supported by a study conducted by Dohrmann and colleagues[4] that found superior math and science performance in high school by children who had attended public Montessori schools, compared to their high school classmates. But that's not all. Two studies by Rathunde and Csikszentmihalyi show a higher level of interest and motivation for school work and more positive social relations among middle school Montessori students when compared to matched controls.[5]

Core Ideas

Table 3.4 shows our rough estimation of how thoroughly Montessori schools have implemented the core ideas described in chapter 2. A description of the core ideas as typically implemented in Montessori follows. For more information on Montessori schools, visit

www.montessori.org/
http://montessori.k12.in.us/programs/index.php
www.montessori.edu/

Core Idea 1: Attainment-Based System

Montessori students work on a task until they master it, and they move on to new tasks when they're ready—both developmentally and with respect to learning prerequisites. Different kinds of assessments are used, depending on the age group and subject area, but assessment is always geared toward mastery; therefore, work is never graded. Assessment is completed primarily through teacher observation of a student during a learning activity, so teaching and testing are fully integrated. This approach improves learning (formative) and certifies attainments (summative).

For subjects such as math, spelling, and grammar, students as young as elementary age use peer collaboration and feedback to further develop their skills. The report card indicates a child's progress in mastering various attainments.

Core Idea 2: Learner-Centered Instruction

Learning experiences in a Montessori classroom are mostly task-based activities designed for individuals to reach specific learning goals. The tasks for younger students typically involve using hands-on learning materials that make abstract concepts clear and concrete. For example, children use beads to develop an understanding of addition, subtraction, multiplication, division, and even exponents at an early age. Fewer hands-on materials are used as students get older, but they still learn by doing.

Table 3.4. Core Ideas in the Montessori System

1. Attainment-based system	Attainment-based student progress	5
	Attainment-based assessment and certifications	5
	Attainment-based student records	5
2. Learner-centered instruction	Customized (personalized) learning	5
	Project-based (task-based) learning	4
	Collaborative learning	2
	Individualized instructional support	5
3. Expanded Curriculum	SCANS curriculum	2
	21st-century skills	3
	All aspects of development	5
4. New Roles	for teachers (guides)	5
	for students	5
	for parents	2
	for technology	0
5. A nurturing school culture	Small school size	5
	Strong relationships	5
	Multiyear mentoring	5
	Multiage grouping	5
	Enjoyable learning	5
	Learning by guides	2
	Family services	0
6. Organizational structures	Schools as clusters	5
	Learning centers	5
	Choice for students	5
	Choice for guides	5
	Administrative structures	NA
	Governance structures	NA
	Ties to other family service systems	1
	A learning cooperative	0

Note: The number indicates the strength of the core idea, with five as highest.

Montessori students typically do not work on the same tasks at the same time; learning is fully customized. Collaborative learning is seldom used in this system, though students have opportunities to collaborate and develop social skills.

Each student in the three-to-five and six-to-eight age groups typically has a weekly work plan that indicates what she will do each day and whether she's done the work. Students in the nine-to-eleven, twelve-to-fourteen, and fifteen-to-eighteen age groups typically have a quarterly work plan.

Some elementary schools use formal conferences with the child, parent, and educator to establish quarterly goals and subjects for work, such as topics for research papers. Children have a major role in deciding what to learn and when—with guidance and encouragement from the educator.

Children with cognitive disabilities and developmental challenges receive the same personalized attention as other students. Rather than mainstreaming children with special education needs into a one-size-fits-all classroom, the opposite happens; regular students enter a customized and highly personalized learning environment similar to the one previously reserved for children with cognitive disabilities.

Core Idea 3: Expanded Curriculum

Montessori curriculum is highly influenced by the Montessori philosophy, which involves cultivating enthusiasm for learning, attending to the development of the whole child, respecting the child, moving from concrete to abstract, using multiaged grouping based on periods of development, and implementing learning-by-doing. The curriculum includes language arts (reading, literature, grammar, creative writing, spelling, and handwriting), mathematics and geometry (such as graphing and story problem solving), cultural subjects (history, geography, science, and research), everyday living skills, sensory awareness exercises, peace education, foreign language instruction, art, music, theater, and movement.

Much of the curriculum is integrated to demonstrate the connections among the different subject areas. Common elements include critical thinking, composition, and research. History lessons link architecture, the arts, science, and technology. And students learn to care about others through community service.

Core Idea 4: New Roles

The teacher's role in a Montessori classroom is described as a "guide on the side" who introduces each child to a new activity when she's ready for it, makes sure the child is using the materials appropriately, and encourages students to make good progress. Since this role is so different from that of a traditional teacher, Montessori organizations prefer the term educator. Even the youngest children (three-year-olds) are helped to be self-directed and work on an activity as long as they are motivated to do so. Visitors who observe a Montessori classroom are often amazed that so many children are deeply absorbed in their respective activities for extended periods.

Montessori students are active learners and largely self-directed after going through a process of "normalization," which entails developing the ability to focus, concentrate, and work independently in an orderly environment that does not disrupt the work of others.

Technology takes the form of hands-on materials that play a central role in each child's learning. These materials provide a task-based environment that simultaneously teaches and tests. At higher age levels, students use computers to access the Internet as a resource and to use word processing for writing reports. Computers in the Montessori system are seldom used for recordkeeping, creating personal learning plans, or assessment. Records and personal learning plans are typically kept on paper, including punch cards, while assessment is done through educator observation and review of student products.

Core Idea 5: A Nurturing School Culture

Montessori schools are small, caring learning environments that facilitate strong, respectful relationships between students and educators and among students. Educators cultivate intrinsic motivation in their pupils, who are grouped into multiage classes that span about three years based on developmental levels. There is early childhood (ages three to five), lower elementary (ages six to eight), upper elementary (ages nine to eleven), middle school (ages twelve to fourteen), and high school (ages fifteen to eighteen). In most cases, each student has the same educators for an entire developmental level (multiyear mentoring).

Core Idea 6: Organizational Structures and Incentives

Montessori educators in many communities are professionals who run their own small school (similar to a cluster as described in chapter 2)—often without a principal. This was the case at the Bloomington Montessori School in Bloomington, Indiana, for many years. This school now has a principal, but his role is primarily that of a public relations contact and administrative manager. The head educator for each age group makes the decisions about curriculum and instruction.

Learning centers are set up within the classroom to focus on certain subjects, such as language arts, everyday living skills, and geography. In each of these areas, materials that support active, hands-on learning are on open display, and the area is set up to facilitate student discussion and stimulate some collaborative learning, as well as individual activity.

Many Montessori schools are private (some are public schools), so parents typically choose to send their child to the school. Parents and students also provide regular feedback to educators. This creates a client-based decision-making system rather than a bureaucratic decision-making system. If a school is not meeting student needs, parents "vote with their feet," just like customers in any other business. These features help make the school a learning organization in which change is continuous.

Some Montessori schools have a board of directors made up chiefly of parents. The board may assume some administrative responsibilities. For example, at the Bloomington Montessori school one board member was the treasurer, who worked with a paid bookkeeper; another was the personnel chair who organized the hiring and employing of all staff in the school; another was the maintenance chair, who either fixed things or contracted the right person to make repairs; a fundraising chair and a long-range planning chair also contributed important skills. But even if they are not involved on the board, parents of Montessori students are often actively involved in decision making for their child.

Some Montessori schools have relationships with local social service agencies, mostly to collaborate on matters of health and parenting skills.

Cost-Effectiveness

Montessori schools have very low administrative costs because they typically do not have a principal or any district office to support. The owners of the school typically teach as well as manage the school. Also, the large role that materials play in the educational process allows customized learning at costs that are typically lower per student than in public schools at the same level.

Related Readings

Hainstock, Elizabeth G. *The Essential Montessori: An Introduction to the Woman, the Writings, the Method, and the Movement.* New York: New American Library, 1978.

Lillard, Angeline S. *Montessori: The Science behind the Genius.* New York: Oxford University Press, 2005.

Montessori, Maria. *The Absorbent Mind.* New York: Holt, Rinehart and Winston, 1967.

———. *The Montessori Method.* New York: Schocken Books, 1964.

Standing, E. Mortimer. *Maria Montessori: Her Life and Work.* New York: New American Library, 1962.

OTHER INFORMATION AGE SCHOOL SYSTEMS

The three Information Age education systems that are described in this chapter are only a few examples out of hundreds of different ways educators are implementing the Information Age paradigm in the United States. Appendix A shows a list of other schools that have adopted many of the core ideas of the Information Age paradigm of education. If you know of any other school systems that score high on these criteria, please send as thorough a description as you can to reigelut@indiana.edu.

CHAPTER SUMMARY OF KEY IDEAS

Table 3.5 summarizes the core ideas implemented in each of the three school systems described in this chapter.

Table 3.5. Summary of Core Ideas in Each School System

Core Idea	Sub-Category of Core Idea	1	2	3
Attainment-based system	Attainment-based student progress	5	5	5
	Attainment-based assessment and certification	5	5	5
	Attainment-based student records	5	5	5
Learner-centered instruction	Customized (personalized) learning	5	5	5
	Project-based (task-based) learning	5	3	4
	Collaborative learning	3	1	2
	Individualized instructional support	5	4	5
Expanded Curriculum	SCANS curriculum	4	1	2
	21st century skills	4	2	3
	All aspects of development	5	4	5
New Roles	for teachers (guides)	5	5	5
	for students	5	5	5
	for parents	4	1	2
	for technology	3	4	0
A nurturing school culture	Small school size	5	5	5
	Strong relationships	5	4	5
	Multi-year mentoring	5	5	5
	Multi-age grouping	5	5	5
	Enjoyable learning	5	3	5
	Learning by guides	3	5	2
	Family services	0	0	0
Organizational structures	Schools as clusters	5	3	5
	Learning centers	3	0	5
	Choice for students	5	2	5
	Choice for guides	5	3	5
	Administrative structures	NA	2	NA
	Governance structures	NA	2	NA
	Ties to other human service systems	4	4	1
	A learning cooperative	0	0	0

Key:

1 = Minnesota New Country School

2 = Chugach School District

3 = Montessori system

NOTES

1. COSN (retrieved March 2010). *Chugach School District: Rural response to local expectations.* Consortium for School Networking Initiative. (http://3d2know.cosn.org/best_practices/chugach.html)

2. Performance criteria include high standards, small and safe environments, teachers working together, strong principal leadership, a focus on student learning, technology to enhance achievement, results oriented, and strong partnerships.

3. Angeline Lillard and Nicole Else-Quest, "The Early Years. Evaluating Montessori Education," *Science* 313, no. 5795 (September 2006): 1893–94.

4. Kathryn R. Dohrmann, Tracy K. Nishida, Alan Gartner, Dorothy K. Lipsky, and Kevin J. Grimm, "High School Outcomes for Students in a Public Montessori Program," *Journal of Research in Childhood Education* 22 (2007): 205–17.

5. Kevin R. Rathunde and Mihály Csikszentmihalyi, "Middle School Students' Motivation and Quality of Experience: A Comparison of Montessori and Traditional School Environments," *American Journal of Education* 111, no. 3 (May 2005): 341–71; Kevin R. Rathunde and Mihály Csikszentmihalyi, "The Social Context of Middle School: Teachers, Friends, and Activities in Montessori and Traditional School Environments," *The Elementary School Journal* 106, no. 1 (September 2005): 59–79.

4

How to Get There from Here

How can the United States move from the Industrial Age paradigm of education to the Information Age system that students and communities need in the modern world? Such fundamental change is far more difficult and risky than piecemeal reforms within an existing paradigm; consequently, the how-to is a very important aspect of this transformation. Knowing how to begin transforming U.S. education systems requires an understanding of alternative *strategies* for the paradigm change process, *principles* that can guide that process, and *open questions* about issues that appear to have no easy answers.

The good news is that some valuable knowledge has already been developed about the paradigm change process by researchers.[1] For example, since 1992, Francis Duffy and Charles Reigeluth have been integrating the work of many practitioner-scholars into a knowledgebase called the School System Transformation Protocol. The two researchers have also been field-testing and improving this knowledgebase in the Metropolitan School District of Decatur Township, a small school district in Indianapolis. District-wide paradigm change has been achieved by the Chugach School District in Alaska (see chapter 3) as well. Tools to support paradigm change are described in appendix C.

STRATEGIES FOR THE PARADIGM CHANGE PROCESS

In this section, we describe two major strategies for creating paradigm change. One centers on transforming existing schools, the other on designing new schools. The latter, designing a new school from scratch, is easier than transforming an existing school because one is able to:

- hire teachers with a mental model that's consistent with the Information Age paradigm, rather than having to help current teachers evolve their mental models
- create a new culture, rather than having to try to change the current culture
- establish new patterns of behavior (for teachers, students, and administrators), rather than having to eradicate old patterns and support new patterns of behavior
- attract students and parents who want the Information Age paradigm of education, rather than having to help students and parents to evolve their mental models
- select or create facilities and resources that are consistent with the new paradigm, rather than having to remodel existing facilities and replace current resources with appropriate ones

While building the desired environment from scratch is easier, having the luxury of starting from scratch is rare.

Within each of the two major paradigm-change strategies are several approaches based on the scale of the effort. These approaches include individual charter schools, school districts, and state departments of education, which we describe in this section.

Charter School

Designing a single school is the small-scale approach to paradigm change, which also makes it the quickest and easiest. However, this approach does not work with individual schools within a school district, because schools in a district are strongly interconnected with other schools in the district (called their peer systems) and the larger systems they serve, such as the school district and community (called their suprasystems).

In other words, a school's connection with the central office and other schools in the district are strong, and a school with a different paradigm from the rest of its district is incompatible with the other elements in the district. Pressure is strong for innovative schools to revert to the predominant paradigm. This is one reason that so many exciting model schools, such as the Saturn School of Tomorrow in St. Paul, Minnesota, and the Microsoft School of the Future in New York City, have reverted back to the Industrial Age paradigm (see "Related Websites" at the end of this chapter).

One way to get around this dynamic is to loosen the bonds between the school and its suprasystems, which is what charter schools do. Charter schools have the freedom to be different. Unfortunately, few take advantage of this opportunity, opting instead to make piecemeal changes within the Industrial Age paradigm. But existing charter schools *can* be transformed, and new charter schools *can* be designed from scratch. The Minnesota New Country School (described in chapter 3) and the Robert Frost Charter School, founded and currently under the direction of one of this book's authors, are examples of charter schools that were created specifically to offer a paradigm of education better suited to meeting today's student needs, and many of the new paradigm schools listed in appendix A are charter schools.

This small-scale approach is the quickest to complete, making it an ideal option for providing a "proof of concept" for funding a larger-scale paradigm change and to conduct research and development to advance the effectiveness of the new paradigm (to move it further up its S-curve of development, as described in chapter 1).

School District

The medium-scale approach is to design a new school district that operates according to the Information Age paradigm. Because the connection between a school district and its suprasystem (state education department) and peer systems (other school districts) are relatively weak, a school district can be of a different paradigm without strong forces pulling it back to the Industrial Age paradigm, particularly if some waivers of state regulations are allowed.

The creation of a brand-new school district is rare, so the most common strategy for this approach is to transform an existing school district, which can be done in one of two ways, based on the size of the district:

- *Small District*: The entire district can undergo transformation, as happened with the CSD in Alaska (described in chapter 3) and as is happening in the Indianapolis Metropolitan School District of Decatur Township in Indiana and the Adams 50 School District in Colorado. This approach is feasible only for small school districts (those having just one high school), because larger districts are more complex.
- *Large District*: A "charter district" strategy works for larger school districts in which the existing school board charters a new district—with its own superintendent, central office, and schools—to operate according to the new paradigm. The charter district must be small—a single high

school and all the schools that feed students into it. The charter district's budget is exactly the same per pupil as the traditional district, and the new district typically uses existing district facilities, personnel, and even some services, such as bussing.

Teachers and administrators in the traditional district must apply to the new district and be selected in order to transfer over. This new, parallel system can start small and gradually bring in more teachers and facilities as subsystems are developed, bugs are worked out, and teachers and parents see its merits.

Either way, transformation must occur in the central office and in all schools within a "feeder system" in the school district (all those schools that feed students into a single high school), because a feeder system has relatively few linkages with other feeder systems, resulting in less leverage being exerted by those systems to change the transformed one back to what it was.

State Department of Education

The large-scale approach is to charge the state education agency, typically called a department of education, with overseeing school districts' transformation to the Information Age paradigm, through either a whole-district or charter-district strategy. This approach is motivated by the recognition that school districts lack both the expertise and the resources to engage in a successful paradigm change effort.

The large-scale approach begins with a "transformational dialogue" among state leaders about the nature of, and need for, paradigm change in public education. An example of this dialogue took place in Ohio under the leadership of the KnowledgeWorks Foundation. It includes all state-level leaders who have a stake in public education, including the governor, legislative leaders, education association leaders (for teachers, administrators, and school boards), business leaders, and postsecondary education leaders.

The transformational dialogue results in a commitment (including legislation) to create a semiautonomous "transformation" unit within or independent of the department of education. The purpose of this unit is to provide resources and experienced facilitators to help school districts that are ready to transform to the new paradigm.

This approach is the most complex and lengthy one of the three we describe in this chapter, but it is the only one that can impact a state system broadly and provide the expertise and resources necessary for a successful district-wide transformation.

PRINCIPLES FOR THE PARADIGM CHANGE PROCESS

In most cases, people approach change with the intent to keep what is good and change what is bad. But when faced with those rare situations in which *paradigm* change is needed, it's essential to think in terms of total change, a transformation, rather than piecemeal change, or reform. Imagine if, at the dawn of the Industrial Age, people thought in terms of improving the horse and wagon instead of developing the railroad! Of course, the railroad of today is not the same as the railroad back then. Piecemeal change has been important for moving the railroad up its S-curve, and it will be equally important for the new paradigm of education.

This fundamental challenge—to think in terms of paradigm change—underlies the principles described in this section: mindset change; consensus-building; broad stakeholder ownership, invention; ideal design; leadership and political support; readiness, capacity, and culture; systemic leverage; change-process expertise; time and money; and technology. These principles are based on the paradigm change experience at the Indianapolis Metropolitan School District of Decatur Township (2001 to 2013) and are informed by research on systemic change in education and business organizations. Also, some tools for paradigm change are described in appendix C.

The Mindset Change Principle

A *mindset* is a collection of mental models that represent a particular perspective. A new paradigm requires a mindset change among stakeholders about what an education system is like. For example, teachers who function as a "sage on the stage" think about teaching and learning much differently than does the "guide on the side" (see chapter 2). And the sorting-focused mentality of the Industrial Age education system is antithetical to a learning-focused mentality needed in the modern world, as explained in chapter 1.

Changes in mindset from an Industrial Age worldview of education to an Information Age worldview are likely *the* most important result of a paradigm change effort, for two reasons:

- First, implementing the Information Age paradigm of education is impossible without a change in mindset among teachers, students, administrators, parents, and community members, because all of these groups have different roles in the new paradigm. To perform these roles, people need to understand how they fit into the education process, what their contributions need to be for its success, and why their particular contributions are important.

- Second, those whose mindsets do not change will resist transformation to the new paradigm, resulting in failure of the change process.

Therefore, the process of transforming our current educational systems must be a learning process—one of helping stakeholders to evolve their mindsets or worldviews about education. In the case of the design-a-new-school strategy, it is usually possible to select teachers and administrators with appropriate mindsets, rather than having to help them evolve their current mindsets. As with the civil rights movement in the 1960s, mindset change is crucial to changes in attitudes and behaviors. Such change cannot be mandated.

The Consensus-Building Principle

One of the most effective ways to help people learn and evolve their mindsets about education is to use a consensus-building process for making decisions about both the new system and the change process. In consensus building, participants learn about new ideas and discuss them with other stakeholders to understand why some others think differently about those ideas, openly exploring the assumptions underlying their thoughts and the merits of alternatives. This process helps participants to evolve their mental models about education and develop shared understandings on which to make decisions, and this leads to a better design that meets student needs.

The consensus-building process for making decisions stands in contrast to the Industrial Age autocratic decision-making process. It is even markedly different from a democratic decision-making process. "Majority rule" creates winners and losers; it creates a minority that is discontent and adversarial. Resistance and sabotage inevitably result. And democratic decision-making is not a learning process; it operates from people's current knowledge and mindsets. For paradigm change in complex systems, this does not work well.

The Broad Stakeholder Ownership Principle

Because change in mental models is so important to successful paradigm change, many stakeholders must be involved in the change process; only through participation can mental models evolve. Furthermore, diverse perspectives enhance the creativity and effectiveness of the invention process.

Beyond stakeholder involvement, their *ownership* of the change process engenders true commitment, reduces resistance to change, and enhances sustainability. Because individual stakeholders have different values about, and views of, what is important in education, empowering stakeholders to own the change can generate discord and increase divisiveness unless processes are in place to build and sustain consensus. That's why cultivating stakeholder ownership requires a different paradigm of leadership (described in the upcoming "The Leadership and Political Support Principle"). It requires building trust, openness, and transparency.

A good first step to building such ownership is to form a team comprised of top opinion leaders from all stakeholder groups in the school system, including the disenfranchised, to lead the paradigm change effort.

In sum, broad stakeholder ownership and a consensus-building process help stakeholders to evolve their mental models about education. Since the transformation process is first and foremost a *learning process*, these principles are crucial to the success of a paradigm change effort.

The Invention Principle

The Information Age paradigm of education is at the same stage of development as air transportation was in 1927, when the Wright Brothers had already proven that the concept of air travel was feasible—Charles Lindberg had just flown across the Atlantic Ocean. The need for air travel was gradually becoming clear, because time-savings were more highly valued by business and political leaders. But much invention remained to be done.

Similarly, in education, evidence shows that the learner-centered paradigm is feasible and needed. Schools are operating early versions of the new paradigm and achieving results that, in many respects, are already better than those of the Industrial Age paradigm (see chapter 3). But we still need to further develop and adapt the various parts of the system to work most effectively and efficiently.

It's not enough to merely adopt the best of what others are doing because different communities have different needs and conditions to address. What works well in one community may not work well in another.

For both these reasons, adopting a "comprehensive school design" or model developed by outsiders of a community is not going to get the job done. Instead, the new paradigm in each community must be designed by the stakeholders there. Invention should consider and build upon what educators have already created elsewhere, but parents, students, community members, and educators must evolve their current mental models about education and construct a new system that genuinely meets their needs.

The Ideal Design Principle

Inventing a new paradigm of education is resisted for two main reasons.

1. Stakeholders have a natural tendency to want to adopt the best of what is out there and skip the process of thinking about *their own* ideal.
2. Educators are practical people and tend to think of the ideal as unrealistic and therefore a waste of time.

An effective way to overcome these challenges is to ask stakeholders to imagine there are no schools and they need to create an ideal learning experience. Ask them to imagine themselves as ten-year-olds and describe how they would want to learn. This is an important approach. When people brainstorm and let go of practicalities, they usually consider options that may have never before come up. This promotes learning, mindset change, and invention. Later, groups can adjust the ideal ideas as necessary to implement the new system but also keep evolving it toward the ideal. What often happens is that ideas previously deemed "pie in the sky" become possible.

Since the learner-centered paradigm can take many different forms, a community should decide on its ideal, look for an existing system that comes closest to that ideal, and then invent adaptations that bring their system even closer to the ideal.

The Leadership and Political Support Principle

Stakeholder ownership and the consensus-building style of decision making both require a different paradigm of leadership. The Industrial Age's supervisory, top-down, command-and-control paradigm isn't productive in the new system (as discussed in chapter 2) or the paradigm change process. The Information Age calls for a leadership style that builds a shared vision among all stakeholders, empowers participants to pursue that shared vision, supports that pursuit, and provides professional development and other resources whenever needed.

This approach generates creativity in how changes are designed and commitment to new designs. Sometimes called *servant leadership*, this is the Information Age paradigm of leadership.

To a large extent, having the right kind of leaders (superintendent and school board members) in place is a "readiness factor" (see next principle) that can determine whether or not a system is prepared for the paradigm change process. If readiness is low, steps can be taken to improve this. An external facilitator can work with the superintendent, school board, and other influential people in the district to develop their understanding of paradigm change, the paradigm change process, and the servant leadership style.

Whether transforming an existing school system or starting a new one, political support is also important. Current school districts are run by elected and appointed leaders who must be convinced to support the paradigm change; without their support, it will fail. Political support must be addressed by helping the superintendent, school board, teacher leaders, and other influential people in the district to understand what paradigm change is, why it is needed, and what it takes to make it happen.

The Readiness, Capacity, and Culture Principle

Given the difficulty of paradigm change, it should not be undertaken until a school system has reached a certain level of readiness and capacity. Culture is an essential part of both readiness and capacity for the paradigm change process. Fundamental change creates certain shifts in culture; yet a certain kind of culture must be in place in order for systemic transformation to happen in the first place.

Some of the most important elements of a culture for paradigm change include appropriate attitudes about empowerment, inclusion, consensus building, collaboration, systems thinking, trust, transparency, and no blame. These elements of culture are also important features of the Information Age paradigm of education.

But readiness and capacity for paradigm change go beyond an appropriate culture. Empowerment of stakeholders requires building an understanding of servant leadership and a high level of trust among stakeholders. Other essential aspects of readiness and capacity include knowing how to think about systems, engage in ideal design, make consensus-based decisions, operate as part of a group process, and understand the concepts of continuous improvement and sustainability. There must be sufficient capacity building before paradigm change is undertaken.

The Systemic Leverage Principle

In a complex system, parts work in an interconnected way. A fundamental change to one part of the system makes it incompatible with the other parts, which then try to change it back to what it was. In fact, one of the reasons that so many promising model schools, like the much-touted Saturn School of Tomorrow in St. Paul, Minnesota, reverted back to the Industrial Age paradigm is because it had become incompatible with the larger, interconnected system.

One way to avoid this is to change all the parts at once. However, creating a complete design or blueprint for such a complex system is difficult, expensive, and time-consuming. An alternative is to choose a few fundamental features to change that exert a lot of pressure on the remaining parts of the old system to change—more pressure than those remaining parts exert on the new parts to revert. In other words, the initial changes must have enough leverage to move the system to what Malcolm Gladwell calls the "tipping point"—where the changes become sustainable and the remaining changes emerge as they are found helpful to support the initial changes.

High-leverage changes in education might include the assessment system (from norm-referenced to criterion-referenced), the student advancement system (from time-based to attainment-based), the planning system (from teacher lesson plans to student personal learning plans), and the teacher's role (from sage-on-the-stage to guide-on-the-side). After such high-leverage changes are made, additional changes gradually emerge as needed to support the initial changes.

The Change Process Expertise Principle

Many educators know how difficult it is to implement piecemeal reform in schools. Yet paradigm change is far more difficult and complex than piecemeal change, because its scope is much larger and the change requires new mindsets, consensus building, invention, a new paradigm of leadership, new roles for stakeholders, and high levels of readiness and capacity in a school community. Because of the greater complexity and difficulty of this change process, guidance by a facilitator who's experienced in paradigm change is important to the success of the transformation process.

Also, stakeholders in a district typically have a long history of disagreements, factions, animosities, rivalries, and such. To neutralize these dynamics, the facilitator must be viewed as impartial by all stakeholder groups, which usually means the person needs to be an outsider. Once appointed, the facilitator is available to facilitate all meetings in the district until an internal person or group can be developed to assume increasing amounts of that role.

As the facilitator role fades out for the initial person in this position, her coaching role grows so the school system can take advantage of that person's experience during the remainder of the paradigm change process.

The Time and Money Principle

Invention and mindset change are time-consuming; they require many stakeholders to be exposed to new ideas and then engage in small-group discussions. Yet time is a precious commodity in schools. Good teachers and administrators are already working overtime and cannot afford to spend much time on a transformation effort. This problem is sometimes likened to trying to redesign an airplane while it is in flight.

One way to handle this problem is to buy out a portion of people's time, which requires money—also in short supply in schools. For example, teachers, administrators, and parent and community leaders could be paid to work on paradigm change during vacations and occasional weekends during the school year.

Without substantial external funding, a paradigm change process can drag on for decades—with outcomes becoming less certain as time goes on due to changes in key personnel and other factors. And this is just for the redesign process! Training teachers for new roles, redesigning facilities, and other retooling expenses also require large amounts of time and money. Without sufficient resources, the transformation process is likely to fail. State governments can play a huge role in addressing these problems, as discussed in chapter 5.

The Technology Principle

The Information Age paradigm requires a more extensive use of technology than the Industrial Age system in order to support customized, learner-centered teaching—cost-effectively. In chapter 2 we describe four major roles of technology for student learning in the new paradigm: recordkeeping, planning, instruction, and assessment. Such extensive use of computers can greatly increase student and teacher productivity, but it requires financial investment in equipment and teacher training. Investment and training are critical to the success of the transformation process.

In sum, here are the fundamental principles for the paradigm-change process in educational systems:

- mindset change
- consensus building
- stakeholder ownership
- invention
- ideal design
- leadership and political support
- readiness, capacity, and culture
- change-process expertise
- time and money
- systemic leverage
- technology

Sidestepping any of these fundamental principles in a paradigm change effort is a near-certain way to eliminate its chances for success.

OPEN QUESTIONS

Some important aspects of the paradigm change process remain open questions; no universal principles appear to exist for them. These questions convey a sense of the complexity of this kind of change process and the extent to which the process must vary from one kind of school or district to another.

Here are a few open questions:

What should change first: beliefs or behaviors?

A convincing case can be made that beliefs must change before behaviors. If a teacher does not understand the role of guide-on-the-side, how can that teacher behave effectively in the new paradigm? Appropriate beliefs and skills appear to be vital for paradigm change to succeed.

On the other hand, forcing a change in behaviors can have a powerful influence on changing beliefs. If you force teachers to use criterion-referenced assessment, continuous student progress, and collaborative project-based learning, they are likely to recognize that this approach is better for students. But this approach requires a significant amount of coaching and other kinds of support.

Here are the merits of each approach:

1. *Voluntary.* If you begin with beliefs, then change is voluntary. Teachers change their behaviors when their beliefs have changed, so they are not forced to change their behaviors.
2. *Time and money.* Fostering change in a teacher's beliefs can require a lot of time and effort. Requiring changes in behaviors is likely to be quicker and less expensive.
3. *Commitment.* Mandating change may create resistance to the changes, either overt or covert. Building changes on new beliefs generates commitment to the new system. And commitment may be crucial when it's important for the teacher to invent new practices for the new paradigm.
4. *Skills.* In both approaches, training in the skills could be provided before teachers change their behaviors. However, the skills may be more difficult to acquire when they are not supported by appropriate beliefs and mindsets.

Therefore, it seems that "beliefs first" might be the best approach when invention is required and teacher resistance or morale could sabotage performance. But "behaviors first" might be preferable when shortage of time and resources threaten to derail the change effort and when teacher mindsets are already somewhat amenable. But perhaps there is a combination approach in which beliefs and behaviors could be addressed simultaneously. This "both–and" thinking might be the best approach of all.

Should stakeholders develop the ideal vision or just buy into it?

One approach to creating an ideal vision is to include many stakeholders from all stakeholder groups in the process of developing it. Here are the advantages of a participatory approach:

1. *More input.* With more people contributing ideas and perspectives, the resulting vision is likely to be stronger.
2. *Mindset change.* Including more people in the process of developing the ideal vision means more people's mindsets about education will change, and mindset change is the most important factor for successful paradigm change. Buy-in and participation also build greater acceptance and capability for change in each stakeholder.
3. *Stronger commitment.* Those who contribute to the development of the vision are likely to feel a deeper sense of ownership and commitment to the vision. This feeling of ownership is important for managing the tough times of the paradigm change process.

An alternative to the two extremes of participate or buy in is for a small group of leaders to develop the ideal vision and then take it to many stakeholders to tweak and build ownership. Among the advantages of this approach are the following three considerations:

1. *Quicker.* The fewer people you involve in building the vision, the less time it takes to reach consensus.
2. *More complete.* Assuming you have the right people involved, the vision is more likely to represent a complete paradigm change rather than a partial (piecemeal) change if you include fewer people with the needed expertise.
3. *More detailed.* A small group of people (typically under a dozen) is likely to build a more detailed vision that provides better guidance for changes in each school than a larger group would create, because it is harder to reach consensus on details in a larger group.

In the Decatur Township change process, for example, the thirty-member Leadership Team's initial ideal vision still had some Industrial Age thinking in it and was very general in the guidance it provided. But this vision paved the way for a more complete ideal vision that was designed several years later.

Given the inadequacy of thinking in terms of either/or, we can look at this issue as a continuum—from only one person developing the ideal vision to every single stakeholder in the school district participating in its development. The question then becomes, how many stakeholders should be involved? This leads to the question, which stakeholders should be involved?

The answer to how many depends on the school district's size, cohesiveness, diversity, urgency for change, and receptivity to new ideas. The answer to which stakeholders depends on the individual's power, influence, creativity, flexibility in thinking, and understanding of Information Age educational needs and realities.

Should the entire school (or district) change at once or in phases?

The essential problem with this issue is that people in all stakeholder groups are arrayed on a continuum—from innovators and early adopters of change to laggards and resisters to any type of change, according to research by Everett Rogers, a pioneering expert in ways that innovations take hold. Some teachers understand and want paradigm change; others need to be dragged into it, and they're kicking and screaming the entire way. Most are somewhere in between. The same is true for parents, administrators, board members, and even students.

So why not divide the school district into two *parallel systems* that operate independently of each other (except for the school board)? Each school building could be divided into two separate "small learning communities," each with its own principal or director. (Often there is an assistant principal in a school, so the number of administrators in the building need not increase.) The central administration could even be divided into two administrations, because the administrative focus in the Industrial Age paradigm is on control, while the focus in the Information Age paradigm is on support. Some offices in the central administration (such as accounting, buildings and grounds, food service, and compliance with state and federal regulations) could serve both systems.

In this setup, teachers, students, and administrators could gradually migrate from the Industrial Age paradigm to the Information Age paradigm in phases as their thinking evolves and they recognize the benefits of the new system.

Here are the advantages of the phased (or parallel systems) approach over the "all at once" approach:

1. *Choice.* Nobody is forced to change. This reduces resistance, particularly among teachers, parents, and other critical stakeholders.
2. *Resources.* Paradigm change involves "retooling" expenses. For instance, details of the new system need to be worked out; teachers need to be trained for new roles; facilities need to be reconfigured and remodeled; and different tools and learning resources need to be acquired. These investments require time, money, and expertise—resources that are in very short supply in many school districts. Spreading out these resource needs over time can be helpful.
3. *Commitment.* Paradigm change can be difficult for teachers because it requires them to develop new skills, acquire new tools, and create new learning resources. A lot of trial and error, learning from mistakes, is typically involved with major change.

The first teachers to change in a district are trailblazers who make the journey of change easier for the pioneers who follow; the early adopters develop resources and work out the major bugs in the instructional, assessment, and recordkeeping systems. The teachers on the innovator end of the continuum have the deepest commitment and best understanding to succeed as trailblazers. Forcing teachers on the opposite end of the continuum to change right away, before these initial issues are worked out, is likely to create resistance, frustration, and duplication of effort and mistakes.

Changing the entire school or district (all teachers and administrators) at once also has some advantages:

1. *Balance.* What if more students want the new paradigm than teachers? This could have serious political repercussions for the phased approach.
2. *Immediacy.* If we know the current system is failing students and the new system will serve them better, why allow some students to continue in the inferior system? The new approach can help all students now.
3. *Equity.* It is possible that the teachers on the innovator side of the continuum are the better teachers. If this is true, then some of the students (possibly the most disadvantaged ones) are left with a lower-quality educational experience in the phased approach. This could be mitigated by having an equal percentage of innovative teachers in every school building and offering equal choice to all students. It would be necessary to compensate for parents who don't care about their child's education or don't take the time to choose wisely.

In sum, it seems that the phased (or parallel systems) approach might be best when the school district is large, has some divisiveness or polarization, and has a high urgency for some to change but low urgency for all to change.

Should you import a model or invent your own?

Some educational models (or school designs) are available that represent important core ideas of the Information Age paradigm—or at least a good step in that direction. Models include Montessori, EdVisions, Big Picture Learning, Reinventing Schools Coalition, New Tech High, Expeditionary Learning, and CoNect systems.

Here are some advantages to importing such a model:

1. *Convenience.* All the design work is done for you. Methods and resources to foster learning have already been developed; tools for managing the learning process have been created; and training programs for teachers are usually readily available.
2. *Time.* All of the convenience factors result in a shorter implementation time for the new system.
3. *Validation.* The methods and resources have typically gone through many cycles of trial and improvement, which verifies that they work well.

Yet there are advantages to inventing your own model. Of course, this approach does not preclude you from utilizing parts of models that others have developed.

1. *Commitment and understanding.* When teachers collaborate to design their own system, they develop a level of commitment to and understanding of the system that's unrivaled by any other approach.
2. *Localized.* A system that's custom designed for a specific school district better meets the needs of the community, students, and teachers that will use the system.
3. *Complete.* Most existing models are an early, incomplete version of the Information Age paradigm. There is no guarantee that a homegrown model will be more complete, but teachers can carefully analyze the current models and incorporate valuable aspects of each in their own design, resulting in a system that likely comes closer to their district's ideal vision than any of the "off-the-shelf" models.

In an attempt to move beyond either/or thinking, frame this issue as a continuum—from adopting an outside model wholesale with no revisions on one extreme and inventing a new model from scratch without utilizing any parts from other models on the other extreme. The question becomes, "Where on the continuum should you be?"

You can, for example, make major revisions to an existing model or combine major elements from two different models. The Robert Frost Charter School in rural New Hampshire blends the Montessori approach to education with project-based learning similar to that used by EdVisions to come up with a model that specifically meets the needs of its community and student population. By developing a program that is closely aligned to the goals and values of the community, Robert Frost Charter School was able to garner the support of key leaders who became important advocates during the school's startup phase.

Over the next few years, more invention is likely to be needed, but as a greater variety of models becomes better developed, relatively less invention will be needed.

How much of your new school should be predesigned?

One approach to paradigm change is to create a thorough design before any implementation—to plan all features of the new school before implementing anything. Another approach is to allow the design to gradually emerge—to start with the core ideas in a district's ideal vision and allow the features of the new school to emerge through trial and error.

Here are some advantages of the thorough design approach:

1. *Fewer mistakes.* If you carefully think through all the features of a new school before implementing them, you are more likely to avoid problems that you would encounter in emergent design. This means fewer frustrations for teachers and a better learning experience for students.
2. *More complete change.* The brainstorming that takes place during a thorough design process is likely to result in a more complete paradigm change than an emergent design approach, because of the tendency to go with what you know or revert to what you're used to when you encounter problems.

On the other hand, there are advantages of emergent design:

1. *Time.* Changes can be implemented in a school much more quickly when using the emergent design approach.
2. *Flexibility.* It is impossible to anticipate all the ways a current school will need to change to become aligned with the district's ideal vision. School systems are just too complex to design completely ahead of time. So why spend a lot of time designing features that you may well end up changing after you try them out?

Again, this question can be reframed as a continuum from thorough to emergent design. Between the extremes is an approach that uses core ideas in your district's ideal vision to design just a few high-leverage structural changes, implements those changes, and then makes additional changes as their benefits become apparent. We call this the *leveraged emergent approach* to paradigm change.

Here are some examples of high-leverage structural changes, which are described in chapter 2:

1. *Attainment-based student progress* requires each student to reach a standard of attainment before progressing to the next one, and it allows each student to progress to the next attainment right after mastering the current one.
2. *Criterion-referenced assessment* replaces the norm-referenced system for monitoring student learning (mastered or not yet mastered).
3. *A record of attainments* replaces the current grades on a report card with a checklist of skills mastered.
4. *A personal learning plan* for every student is a learning contract that describes what will be learned by a given date and the means by which it will be learned, with milestones.
5. *Teacher's role* changes from "sage on the stage" (lecturer) to "guide on the side" (facilitator).
6. *Instructional approach* changes from teacher-centered to learner-centered—where education is self-directed, team-based, and project-based.

Where you choose to begin on this continuum depends to some extent on whether you import a model or invent your own.

CHAPTER SUMMARY OF KEY IDEAS

Strategies for paradigm change include transforming existing schools and designing new schools. Three approaches are available for each of these two strategies based on the scale of the effort:

- *Small scale.* Charter schools have freedom to be a different paradigm. This approach is quickest and easiest, making it ideal to move the paradigm up its S-curve.
- *Medium scale.* School districts have more freedom than individual schools within the district. Small districts should transform the whole district, whereas large districts should charter a district—comprised of a

single high school and all the schools that feed students into it—to operate independently of the rest of the district.

- *Large scale.* State-level change is brought about through a transformational dialogue among state leaders. It produces a semiautonomous "transformation" unit to help school districts that are ready to transform.

Fundamental principles of paradigm change must be addressed for successful transformation. Here are the principles that matter most:

- *Mindset change.* The process must place top priority on helping teachers, students, administrators, parents, and other community members to evolve their mental models about education.
- *Consensus.* Decisions in the change process need to be made by building consensus through learning together and not by a win-or-lose vote system.
- *Stakeholder ownership.* The process must facilitate broad stakeholder ownership in order to engender true commitment, reduce resistance, and enhance sustainability.
- *Invention.* The process must include creating innovative school designs. Invention should consider and build upon what pioneering educators have already created elsewhere.
- *Ideal design.* The process must help stakeholders to think in the ideal about their new educational system.
- *Leadership and political support.* The process must have support and leadership from all formal and informal leaders in the district. The autocratic paradigm of leadership must be replaced by servant leadership, which builds a shared vision and supports all stakeholders in pursuit of it.
- *Readiness, capacity, and culture.* A culture of empowerment, inclusion, consensus building, collaboration, systems thinking, trust, disclosure, and no blame is necessary for the transformation process. Other aspects of readiness include knowing how to think about systems, engage in ideal design, make consensus-based decisions, operate as part of a group process, and understand the concepts of continuous improvement and sustainability.
- *Systemic leverage.* The most impactful structural changes should be made first and then allow the remaining changes to emerge naturally over time.
- *Change process expertise.* An experienced and impartial facilitator must guide the change process, and the role of this facilitator gradually transitions from facilitator to advisor.
- *Time and money.* Individuals need to be available to participate in activities and discussions that help them to shift their mindsets, invent a new system, and implement the changes. And time is money.

- *Technology.* Hardware and software are needed to support customization of student instruction and empower students and teachers to become more autonomous and self-directed.

Open Questions:

- *Which should change first: beliefs or behaviors?* It depends on the situation; but working on them simultaneously might be the best approach.
- *Should stakeholders develop the ideal vision or just buy into it?* The answer to how many and which stakeholders should be involved in developing the ideal vision depends on a variety of factors related to the school district.
- *Should the entire school (or district) change at once or in phases?* The phased (or parallel systems) approach might be best for a large school district, one with divisiveness or polarization, and one with a high urgency for some (but not all) schools to change.
- *Should you import a model or invent your own?* Over the next few years, more models need to be invented than imported; but eventually most models can be imported and little invented.
- *How much of your new school should be predesigned?* Find a reasonable middle point in the continuum between predesign and emergent design. The exact right spot depends to some extent on whether you import a model or invent your own.

NOTE

1. Such researchers include Bela Banathy, Francis Duffy, Phillip Schlechty, Patrick Jenlink, and Charles Reigeluth in the education sector, and Russell Ackoff, Peter Senge, and Hammer and Champy in the corporate sector (see this chapter's related readings).

RELATED READINGS

Ackoff, Russell L. *Creating the Corporate Future.* New York: Wiley, 1981.
Banathy, Bela H. *Systems Design of Education: A Journey to Create the Future.* Englewood Cliffs, NJ: Educational Technology Publications, 1991.
———. *Designing Social Systems in a Changing World.* New York: Plenum Press, 1996.

Duffy, Francis M. *Step-Up-to-Excellence: An Innovative Approach to Managing and Rewarding Performance in School Systems.* Lanham, MD: Scarecrow Education, 2002.

Duffy, Francis M., and Charles M. Reigeluth. "The School System Transformation (SST) Protocol." *Educational Technology* 48, 4 (2008): 41–49.

Duffy, Francis M., Lynda G. Rogerson, and Charles Blick. *Redesigning America's Schools: A Systems Approach to Improvement.* Norwood, MA: Christopher-Gordon Publishers, 2000.

Fullan, Michael. *Leading in a Culture of Change.* San Francisco: Jossey-Bass, 2001.

Gladwell, Malcolm. *The Tipping Point: How Little Things Can Make a Big Difference.* New York: Little, Brown, 2000.

Hammer, Michael. *Beyond Reengineering: How the Process-Centered Organization Is Changing Our Work and Our Lives.* New York: HarperBusiness, 1996.

Hammer, Michael, and James Champy. *Reengineering the Corporation: A Manifesto for Business Revolution.* New York: HarperBusiness, 2001.

Jenlink, Patrick M., ed. *Systemic Change: Touchstones for the Future School.* Arlington Heights, IL: IRI/Skylight Training and Publishing, 1995.

Jenlink, Patrick M., Charles M. Reigeluth, Alison A. Carr, and Laurie M. Nelson. "An Expedition for Change." *Tech Trends* 41, no. 1 (1996): 21–30.

Joseph, Roberto, and Charles M. Reigeluth. "The Systemic Change Process: A Conceptual Framework." *Contemporary Educational Technology* 1, no. 2 (2010): 97–117.

Kim, Daniel H. (2008). *Transformational Dialogue for Public Education: 50-State Strategy.* http://knowledgeworks.org/conversation/ research-and-resources/2/ transformational-dialogue-public-education.

Kotter, John. *Leading Change.* Cambridge, MA: Harvard Business Review Press, 2012.

Reigeluth, Charles M. "Principles of Educational Systems Design." *International Journal of Educational Research* 19, no. 2 (1993): 117–31.

———. "A Leveraged Emergent Approach to Systemic Transformation. *TechTrends* 50 no. 2 (2006): 46–47.

———. "Chaos Theory and the Sciences of Complexity: Foundations for Transforming Education." In *Systems Thinkers in Action: A Field Guide for Effective Change Leadership in Education,* edited by Blane Despres. New York: Rowman & Littlefield, 2008.

Reigeluth, Charles M., and Francis M. Duffy. "The AECT FutureMinds Initiative: Transforming America's School Systems. *Educational Technology* 48, no. 3 (2008): 45–49.

Reigeluth, Charles M., and Don Stinson. "The Decatur Story: Reinvention of a School Corporation—Leadership and Empowerment in Decatur's School Transformation." *The Indiana School Boards Association Journal* 53, no. 2 (2007): 13–15.

Rogers, Everett M. *Diffusion of Innovations,* 3rd ed. New York: Free Press, 1983.

Schlechty, Phillip C. *Schools for the Twenty-first Century: Leadership Imperatives for Educational Reform.* San Francisco: Jossey-Bass, 1990.

———. *Shaking up the Schoolhouse.* San Francisco: Jossey-Bass, 2001.

———. *Working on the Work*. New York: Wiley, 2002.

———. *Creating Great Schools: Six Critical Systems at the Heart of Educational Innovation*. San Francisco: Jossey-Bass, 2005.

Senge, Peter M. *The Fifth Discipline: The Art and Practice of the Learning Organization*. New York: Doubleday, 1990.

———. *Schools That Learn: A Fifth Discipline Fieldbook for Educators, Parents, and Everyone Who Cares about Education*. New York: Doubleday, 2000.

Wagner, Tony, and Robert Kegan. *Change Leadership: A Practical Guide to Transforming Our Schools*. San Francisco: Jossey-Bass, 2006.

RELATED WEBSITES

The Microsoft School of the Future: www.eschoolnews.com/2009/06/01/school-of-the-future-lessons-in-failure/

The Saturn School of Tomorrow: www2.ed.gov/pubs/EdReformStudies/EdTech/saturn.html

5

What Governments Can Do

Eventually, a paradigm change will occur for education systems in the United States, and the performance of the U.S. educational systems will greatly improve—likely at a lower cost per student than our Industrial Age paradigm. But the cost to transform the current systems into the new paradigm is not trivial.

Imagine transportation systems in 1927, when Charles Lindberg had just flown across the Atlantic Ocean. A tremendous amount of research and development was needed to allow passengers and freight to slowly shift over time from trains and ships to airplanes. During World War II, government investment in this R&D greatly accelerated the shift.

Similarly, without public investment in R&D for the new paradigm of education, the shift may be painfully slow. The pain of this process will be felt by educators, who need to make extra effort for the transformation over a long period, as well as by students, communities, and the economy that are being damaged by an outdated educational system (see appendix B).

So, what kinds of public investments are likely to yield the greatest rewards? Would it help to generate more knowledge about both process and product (or means and ends)? The product, or ends, is what the new paradigm should be like, including roles, methods, and tools. The process, or means, is how to transform our current school systems to the new paradigm and develop new school systems of the new paradigm.

We propose four major education initiatives that the federal government could fund:

1. Support the development of open-source technological tools for the Information Age paradigm.

2. Support the piloting of best practices for the Information Age system in charter schools.
3. Help states build the capacity to facilitate the district-wide paradigm change process.
4. Support the creation of knowledge about the paradigm change process.

SUPPORT DEVELOPMENT OF TECHNOLOGICAL TOOLS

In chapter 2 we describe digital technology's role in the Information Age paradigm and compare that role to the minor, peripheral role that such technology plays in the Industrial Age paradigm. The new role includes record-keeping, planning, instruction, and assessment for student learning as well as a variety of communication and administration processes.

Consider motor vehicles as a system of transportation. At first, you may think only of the automobile and its development. But if you dig a little deeper, you probably realize that in order for the automobile of the 1910s to reach the level of performance we have today, affordable fuel needed to become available. Imagine how much R&D has gone into exploration for oil and then drilling, refining, distributing, and retailing gasoline. Think of the infrastructure that needed to be developed—the filling stations, oil refineries, tankers, and pipelines!

Motor vehicles also require good roads. Dirt roads and cobblestone streets were the norm in those early days. A huge amount of research went into asphalt and concrete materials and bridge designs, and enormous investments were made in infrastructure to create our roads and interstate highways. And, yes, government support was crucial. But that's not all. People need a way to maintain and repair automobiles. Repair shops, parts dealers, and parts distribution systems all needed to be developed and improved over time. The list goes on: licensing drivers, insuring automobiles, erecting directional and other types of signs, establishing and enforcing road rules, establishing safety standards, and more. All of these play a part in the establishment and success of the U.S. motor vehicle transportation system.

Yet the Information Age paradigm of education is even more complex than the auto industry, so it requires more R&D to move it up its S-curve toward its upper limit (see chapter 1). We believe strongly that competition and free markets provide valuable incentives for smart investment that is responsive to customers' preferences. Thus, our first instinct was to look to the business community to make the needed investments in infrastructure (the digital machines and software) for the new education paradigm. But rather than deciding on the basis of philosophy or ideology, it is wise to take a pragmatic look at obstacles, options, and consequences.

Prime the pump. First, there is the chicken-and-egg problem: there is so little current investment in educational tools for the Information Age paradigm because there are not enough new paradigm schools to buy them, and there are no more new schools because not enough good tools are available to make the Information Age paradigm feasible. An initial investment in the development of automated digital tools by the public (government) could prime the pump; subsequent investments would come from private firms and end users.

Keep it free. An important characteristic of the Information Age is open (read: free) resources. Think of Linux, an operating system for your computer that's an alternative to Microsoft Windows and Mac OSX. Users contribute to the development of the system, and the system is available for free. Also think of Wikipedia. It is a user-produced encyclopedia that is updated by users and available to all for free. In education, Moodle, Sakai, and eFront are open-source alternatives to course management systems such as Blackboard, CCNet, and Pearson's Pegasus. This is not government competing with businesses; this is users collaborating to compete with businesses. This is Toffler's concept of the prosumer—whereby the consumer is also the producer in the Information Age—that shows great promise for lowering costs in education.

Educational institutions, including MIT and Harvard as well as Florida Open High School and the Utah Open High School, are also creating educational resources and making them available for free on the Internet. So are not-for-profits like the Khan Academy. And teachers at all levels of the educational system are contributing lesson plans and lessons to banks of open educational resources. This pattern of sharing centers on users collaborating to compete with businesses, and it's becoming a viable alternative to the traditional commercial model for software and courseware. This trend has huge implications for developing web-based educational tools and lowering costs for education.

The chicken-and-egg problem is also relevant to open educational resources. A modest public investment at the federal level in the initial development of the architecture and components of open-source systems could make a big difference in how quickly these free educational tools become powerful enough to put more school systems throughout the nation in a position to transform to the new paradigm relatively smoothly. Its effect on education could be even more powerful than the effect of the interstate highway system on the productivity of automobile and truck transportation systems. This kind of investment is clearly more appropriate for the federal government to make than for states, whose efforts would be largely redundant.

SUPPORT PILOTING OF BEST PRACTICES

A major challenge for paradigm change is moving the new system up its S-curve of development as rapidly as possible, which has a significant impact on student learning, the quality of life in communities, and the economic competitiveness of the United States. Timing matters.

In chapter 4 we explain that fundamental change in a school makes it incompatible with the rest of its school district, which works to change it back to the status quo. We indicated that one solution is to view the school district as the unit of change. But it takes much longer to transform a school district to a new paradigm than to transform a single school. Given that time is so important, the best option in many cases may be to transform a charter school, which is free from district pressures to change back.

Unfortunately, few charter schools have taken advantage of their freedom for two main reasons.

- *Lack of vision.* A limited understanding of what the Information Age paradigm is and why it is needed so desperately.
- *Transition costs.* It takes a considerable amount of time and money to install a new system that differs so much from the norm—for which teachers are not prepared and powerful tools have not yet been developed.

So, even though new paradigm schools are likely to be less expensive per student than Industrial Age schools, two kinds of costs come into play that are beyond what most charter schools can bear.

The first is the cost of installing the new paradigm, which includes procuring the needed digital technology tools and providing the professional development that teachers need to perform their new roles.

The second kind of expense is R&D to move the new system up its S-curve and thereby make it easier for other school systems to transform to the new paradigm as well.

A major difficulty with the charter school approach to R&D is that the primary and secondary U.S. educational process spans preschool through twelfth grade—not just K–8 or 9–12. The Information Age paradigm is so different from the factory model of schools that transitioning from one paradigm to the other is going to be very difficult on students. Montessori students provide ample evidence of this, with their difficulties in moving from a self-directed, project-based learning environment where they work on something until they master it, to a teacher-directed, decontextualized, sorting-focused learning environment. So charter schools that participate in this R&D effort should perform the entire educational process for individual students (P–12) or do so in partnership with another charter school.

Some K–8 and 9–12 charter schools have already developed early versions of the new paradigm (see chapter 3 and appendix A). We propose that some of the public charter schools should receive support, on a competitive basis, to research and develop improvements in their tools and practices to make those advancements available to regular public schools as they transform to the learner-centered paradigm. This initiative should be done on the federal level to minimize duplication and maximize communication and collaboration among charter schools that show the most promise.

This kind of public investment could pay huge dividends—not by supporting charter schools but by using charter schools as a vehicle for educational R&D to improve the Information Age paradigm. Without public investment in moving the new paradigm up its S-curve, systemic change will likely occur slowly while students, communities, and the U.S. economy suffer that much longer. The costs of forgoing this R&D initiative no doubt considerably outweigh the amount of public investment needed.

HELP STATES BUILD CAPACITY
TO FACILITATE PARADIGM CHANGE

School districts lack the expertise and resources needed to engage in successful paradigm change. For the following reasons, we think that state education agencies (SEAs), often known as *state departments of education*, are in the best position to function as the primary agents to help school districts change:

1. SEA policies are often major obstacles to paradigm change, so the policies of these agencies must change to help school districts transform to the new paradigm.
2. States have the primary constitutional responsibility for public education.
3. As tax collectors, states have a way to allocate funding to offset the expense of district-level paradigm change.

What is needed for SEAs to assume this role? First, a state must engage in a process whereby state leaders from all major stakeholder groups, including the governor and legislators, engage in "transformational dialogue" to reach consensus about the need for paradigm change. Developing the will and commitment to engage in paradigm change is prerequisite to state actions to support transformation. Since 2007 the KnowledgeWorks Foundation, in collaboration with the National Coalition on Teaching and America's Future, has been facilitating a state-level transformational dialogue process in Ohio that could serve as a national model.

Second, after the will and commitment for paradigm change are developed among state leaders, a state needs to build its SEA's capacity to facilitate district-wide paradigm change, which includes both expertise and resources.

The U.S. Department of Education could facilitate the transformation of the nation's education systems by launching an initiative to help state leaders meet these four initial objectives related to paradigm change in the education system:

1. Engage in a transformational dialogue process.
2. Form and develop a unit in their SEA that is charged solely with facilitating paradigm change in school districts.
3. Change state laws and policies to remove obstacles to paradigm change.
4. Provide funding to help school districts at high levels of readiness to engage in the paradigm change process by offering federal funds to match state funds.

DEVELOPING KNOWLEDGE ON THE PARADIGM CHANGE PROCESS

Paradigm change is far more difficult to implement than piecemeal reforms, yet very little research has been done to advance knowledge about the paradigm change process, perhaps because people know so little about it. More knowledge is needed about how to help people evolve their mindsets about education. More needs to be learned about how to build stakeholder ownership of the change process, how to implement consensus-based decision making, how to help people engage in ideal design, how to help administrators to practice servant leadership, how to help large school districts address their unique obstacles to paradigm change, and much more.

More knowledge is also needed about the design of digital technology tools to support the Information Age paradigm, about how best to train teachers for their new roles and for use of the new tools, and about how to help a district office to transform its practices to a support role rather than a command-and-control role.

Given the lack of knowledge about so many aspects of the paradigm change process, funding is pivotal to advance that knowledge and thereby help school districts engage successfully in the paradigm change process.

A FEDERAL STRATEGY

We have proposed four major education initiatives that the federal government could fund:

1. Support the development of open-source technological tools for the Information Age paradigm.
2. Support the piloting of best practices for the Information Age system in charter schools.
3. Help states build the capacity to facilitate the district-wide paradigm change process.
4. Support the creation of knowledge about the paradigm change process.

By funding these four initiatives, the federal government can dramatically speed up the paradigm change process in the nation's educational systems. We recommend the creation of a "Foundation for Educational Transformation" modeled on the National Science Foundation that would have the autonomy and resources to fund initiatives such as these.

We also recommend a phased approach to each of these four initiatives, which is described next and summarized in table 5.1.

1. Development of Technological Tools

The first phase of this initiative might involve the foundation funding, on a competitive basis, (a) an analysis of the existing technological tools that serve the functions needed for the Information Age paradigm of education, and (b) with that information, the design of an interactive open-source digital technology system that can integrate the four core functions of the education process: recordkeeping, planning, instruction, and assessment for student learning.

The second phase could center on funding the development of the open-source system (as always, through competitive bids whereby organizations submit proposals to do to the work, and the best proposal is funded).

The third phase could fund field testing of this technology system—possibly within charter schools that are transforming to the new paradigm—in an effort to continuously improve and further develop the system. This could be very helpful for schools participating in the second initiative, described next.

2. Pilot Best Practices

In the first phase of this initiative, the foundation could fund the process of identifying charter schools that have made significant strides in adopting the Information Age paradigm. A preliminary list of such schools is shown in appendix A.

In the second phase, some of those charter schools could be supported to further develop their methods, practices, tools, cultures, policies, systems, and teacher skills through formative evaluation. Such evaluation would identify strengths and weaknesses and identify possible ways of overcoming those weaknesses without diminishing the strengths. This will help move the Information Age paradigm up its S-curve of development. The results of this phase could be helpful in the other three initiatives, and these charter schools would be prime candidates to be test sites for the field test of the technology system (initiative one, phase three).

In the third phase, the foundation could provide support to new charter schools for planning and implementing the new paradigm in order to provide them additional opportunities to strengthen the new paradigm.

3. Help States Build Capacity

In the first phase, the foundation could work with two[1] states that are at high levels of readiness to help them engage in a process like the Knowledge-Works Foundation's *Transformational Dialogue for Public Education* in Ohio.[2] This process builds state-level capacity to enact legislation and form an organization, either inside or outside of the SEA, that can facilitate district-wide paradigm change in the state. As part of this program, the foundation would help the states to choose a few school districts of various sizes to lead the charge for paradigm change.

The second phase of this initiative might involve scaling up of the effort to include additional states that are ready to engage in a similar process of state-level paradigm change.

4. Further Knowledge about the Paradigm Change Process

In the initial phase of this initiative, the Foundation might fund a review of current knowledge of two kinds: how to achieve paradigm change in individual school districts and how to build state capacity to facilitate the district-level paradigm change process. This work should precede and inform the first phase of initiatives two and three.

In the second phase of this initiative, the foundation might fund efforts to build on the current knowledge about the paradigm change process by using the design-based research method, which entails working with a school district or state to help them implement the current knowledge about the transformation process for the district or state level, identifying what works well and what doesn't, and trying out ways of improving what doesn't work well in search of improvements that won't diminish the strengths. This kind of research has been conducted in the Indianapolis Metropolitan School District of Decatur Township since January 2001. It could be piggybacked onto the second phase of initiative two and the first phase of initiative three. This research

Table 5.1. Four Government Initiatives and Their Phases

1. Develop technological tools	2. Pilot best practices	3. Help states build capacity	4. Advance knowledge about paradigm change process
1.1 Design an integrated tool	2.1 Identify charter schools	3.1 Work with two states	4.1 Review current knowledge
1.2 Develop the tool	2.2 Evaluate and improve a few of those schools	3.2 Scale up the effort with additional states	4.2 Conduct research to improve current knowledge
1.3 Field test the tool	2.3 Support new charter schools		

should be repeated in cycles that result in ever-improving knowledge about how to transform educational systems to the Information Age paradigm.

Such a phased approach to each initiative allows for development of sufficient knowledge about the transformation process to dramatically improve the success rate and reduce the time required for paradigm change in school districts. And a foundation for educational transformation would greatly facilitate sharing of knowledge and experience among the four initiatives as well as among the participating states and school districts.

Eventually, work needs to be done to develop teacher preparation programs for the dramatically different kind of role that teachers will play in the Information Age paradigm of education, as well as for leadership preparation programs, but the immediate need is for in-service teacher preparation rather than preservice preparation. The foundation would be able to play an important role here, too.

A FINAL WORD

You may be asking, "Can the paradigm change process occur without public investment in it?" Sure! In fact, as Alvin Toffler has argued persuasively in his book, *The Third Wave*, paradigm change in education is inevitable as a part of the huge wave of change represented by the information revolution. The questions are:

1. How long will it take?
2. How much turmoil, pain, and suffering will our educators endure during the paradigm change process?

3. How much damage will be done to our students, communities, and economy in the interim? (See appendix B.)

Without federal funding, progress toward the new paradigm will continue to be slow and sporadic. A careful analysis of all the costs and benefits will show that a significant public investment will pay for itself many times over.

CHAPTER SUMMARY OF KEY IDEAS

Here are four education paradigm change initiatives for the federal government to support:

1. Develop technological tools.
   - "Prime the pump" to spur private investment in technological tools.
   - "Prime the pump" to spur user development of open-source software.
2. Pilot best practices.
   - Charter schools have the systemic independence from a school district to undergo a paradigm change without a school district's old-paradigm structures working against them.
   - Charter schools encounter two costs associated with paradigm change: (1) installing the new paradigm (costs of tools and professional development), and (2) improving the new paradigm with R&D that moves it up its S-curve of development.
   - Charter schools must include all grade levels to span the entire P–12 process of local public education.
   - P–12 charter schools should receive federal support, on a competitive basis, to research and develop improvements in their tools and practices, so that those advancements can make it easier and quicker for regular public schools to transform themselves to the learning-focused paradigm.
3. Build states' capacity to facilitate paradigm change.
   - Most school districts lack both the expertise and the resources to engage in paradigm change.
   - States should be the primary agents in helping school districts to transform themselves to the new paradigm.
   - States require outside facilitation and resources to develop the will and capacity to support school district transformation. Without support from the foundation, it is either unlikely to happen, or it will take a lot longer to occur.
   - State leaders must engage in a transformational dialogue culminating in developing legislation and institutional capacity to help school districts transform themselves.

4. Develop knowledge on the paradigm change process.
   - The paradigm change process is far more difficult and perilous than piecemeal reforms, and more knowledge is needed about how to help systems succeed in transforming themselves to the new paradigm.
   - More knowledge is needed about the design of digital technology to support the new paradigm.
   - Funding to advance knowledge about paradigm change will greatly enhance success in transformation efforts.

A federal strategy can unfold in phases.

1. *Tools.* Phase one to analyze existing tools. Phase two to develop a comprehensive system. Phase three to field-test the system.
2. *Best practices.* Phase one to identify charter schools that best exemplify the Information Age paradigm. Phase two to help some schools further develop their tools and practices. Phase three to help new charter schools implement the new paradigm.
3. *State capacity.* Phase one to help two states engage in transformational dialogue and develop legislation and form an organization to help districts transform themselves. Phase two to scale up the support to other states at high levels of readiness.
4. *Knowledge.* Phase one to review current knowledge about district-level and state-level paradigm change processes. Phase two to conduct R&D in conjunction with the district-level and state-level paradigm change processes applying that knowledge.

Eventually, support for the design of teacher preparation and leadership programs will be helpful.

NOTES

1. It should be more than one, in case one effort gets derailed by local circumstances, but it should not be much more than two, because that would dilute resources that are needed for early successes.
2. Discussed in chapter 4 under "Strategies for the Paradigm Change Process."

RELATED READINGS

Design-Based Research Collective. "Design-Based Research: An Emerging Paradigm for Educational Inquiry." *Educational Researcher* 32, no. 1 (2003): 5–8.

Kim, Daniel H. *Transformational Dialogue for Public Education: 50-State Strategy.* http://knowledgeworks.org/conversation/ research-and-resources/2/ transformational-dialogue-public-education, 2008.

Reigeluth, Charles M., and Francis M. Duffy. "The AECT FutureMinds Initiative: Transforming America's School Systems." *Educational Technology* 48, no. 3 (2008): 45–49.

Reigeluth, Charles M., and Don Stinson. "The Decatur Story: Reinvention of a School Corporation—Mission and Values for Decatur's School Transformation." *The Indiana School Boards Association Journal* 53, no. 1 (2007): 17–19.

Richter, Kurt B. "Integration of a Decision-Making Process and a Learning Process in a Newly Formed Leadership Team for Systemic Transformation of a School District." PhD diss., Indiana University, 2007.

Richter, Kurt, and Charles M. Reigeluth. "Systemic Transformation in Public School Systems." In *Dream! Create! Sustain! Mastering the Art and Science of Transforming School Systems*, edited by Francis M. Duffy, 288–315. Lanham, MD: Rowman & Littlefield Education, 2010.

Schlechty, Phillip C. *Schools for the Twenty-first Century: Leadership Imperatives for Educational Reform.* San Francisco: Jossey-Bass, 1990.

———. *Shaking up the Schoolhouse.* San Francisco: Jossey-Bass, 2001.

Appendix A

Schools Evolving into the Information Age Paradigm

Table A.1 is a list of schools that an Indiana University research team identified as likely to be evolving into the Information Age paradigm of education. It is a tentative list because the research team has only been able to do a preliminary analysis of public information about the schools. The team, led by Dabae Lee, is comprised of Yeol Huh, Chun-Yi Lin, and Charles Reigeluth. Eulho Jung, Mina Min, and Verily Tan have assisted the team.

The table shows the school name, the type of school system (individual school, school district, or national school model), what district or model it is a part of, and the presence or absence of five criteria for the Information Age paradigm: attainment-based student progress, personalized learning, collaborative problem-based learning, criterion-referenced student assessment, and multiage grouping with multiyear mentoring.

The number of such characteristics is added to provide an overall rating of the extent to which the school system can be considered in the Information Age paradigm. However, this does not take into account the greater importance of some criteria over others. Schools are listed alphabetically within rating category, beginning with the ones that have the most Information Age core ideas.

If you know of any schools that should be added to this list, please contact us (reigelut@indiana.edu) to help us improve a website with current information: www.reinventingschools.net.

Table A.1. Schools Evolving into the Information Age Paradigm

Key: Dis = District; Mod = Model; Ind = Individual school

Ref #	School Name	Type	Model or District	Att-bsd S Prog	Pers Lrng	Coll PBL	Crit-ref Assmt	Multiyear/-age	Rating (1-5)
1	Chenega Bay Community School	Dis	Chugach School District	v	v	v	v	v	5
2	Tatitlek Community School	Dis	Chugach School District	v	v	v	v	v	5
3	Whittier Community School	Dis	Chugach School District	v	v	v	v	v	5
4	Aveson School	Mod	EdVisions	v	v	v	v	v	5
5	Family Partnership School	Mod	EdVisions	v	v	v	v	v	5
6	Golden Eagle Charter School	Mod	EdVisions	v	v	v	v	v	5
7	New Haven Youth and Family Services	Mod	EdVisions	v	v	v	v	v	5
8	North County Trade Tech High School	Mod	EdVisions	v	v	v	v	v	5
9	Hakipuu Learning Center	Mod	EdVisions	v	v	v	v	v	5
10	Kickapoo Nation School	Mod	EdVisions	v	v	v	v	v	5
11	Blue Hill Harbor School	Mod	EdVisions	v	v	v	v	v	5
12	Academic Arts High School	Mod	EdVisions	v	v	v	v	v	5
13	Avalon School	Mod	EdVisions	v	v	v	v	v	5
14	Edvision Off Campus	Mod	EdVisions	v	v	v	v	v	5
15	El Colegio Charter School	Mod	EdVisions	v	v	v	v	v	5
16	Harbor City International School	Mod	EdVisions	v	v	v	v	v	5
17	High School for Recording Arts	Mod	EdVisions	v	v	v	v	v	5
18	Minnesota New Country School	Mod	EdVisions	v	v	v	v	v	5
19	New Century Academy	Mod	EdVisions	v	v	v	v	v	5
20	Northern Lights Community School	Mod	EdVisions	v	v	v	v	v	5
21	Northfield School of Arts and Techn.	Mod	EdVisions	v	v	v	v	v	5
22	RiverBend Acad	Mod	EdVisions	v	v	v	v	v	5
23	SAGE Academy	Mod	EdVisions	v	v	v	v	v	5
24	Academy for Independent Studies	Mod	EdVisions	v	v	v	v	v	5
25	Explore Knowledge Academy	Mod	EdVisions	v	v	v	v	v	5

#	School	Type	Affiliation						
26	High Desert Montessori School	Mod	EdVisions	✓	✓	✓	✓	✓	5
27	Resource Link Charter School	Mod	EdVisions	✓	✓	✓	✓	✓	5
28	Propel Andrew Street High School	Mod	EdVisions	✓	✓	✓	✓	✓	5
29	Eagle Harbor High School	Mod	EdVisions	✓	✓	✓	✓	✓	5
30	Phoenix School	Mod	EdVisions	✓	✓	✓	✓	✓	5
31	Rivercity Leadership Academy	Mod	EdVisions	✓	✓	✓	✓	✓	5
32	Spokane Medicine Wheel	Mod	EdVisions	✓	✓	✓	✓	✓	5
33	Birchwood Blue Hills Charter Schl	Mod	EdVisions	✓	✓	✓	✓	✓	5
34	Cooperative Educ. Service Agency #12	Mod	EdVisions	✓	✓	✓	✓	✓	5
35	Crossroads Academy	Mod	EdVisions	✓	✓	✓	✓	✓	5
36	High Marq Environmental Charter School	Mod	EdVisions	✓	✓	✓	✓	✓	5
37	Kornerstone School	Mod	EdVisions	✓	✓	✓	✓	✓	5
38	Northwoods Community Secondary School	Mod	EdVisions	✓	✓	✓	✓	✓	5
39	TAGOS Leadership Academy	Mod	EdVisions	✓	✓	✓	✓	✓	5
40	Valley New School	Mod	EdVisions	✓	✓	✓	✓	✓	5
41	Robert Frost Charter School	Ind	N/A	✓	✓	✓	✓	✓	5
42	Great Expectations School	Ind	N/A	✓	✓	✓	✓	✓	5
43	The Brooklyn Free School	Ind	N/A	✓	✓	✓	✓	✓	5
44	Highland Tech Charter School	Ind	Re-Inventing Schls. Coalition	✓	✓	✓	✓	✓	5
45	Crown Pointe Acad. of Westminster	Dis	Adams County School Distr 50	✓	✓	✓			4
46	Early Childhood Center	Dis	Adams County School Distr 50	✓	✓	✓			4
47	F.M. Day Elementary	Dis	Adams County School Distr 50	✓	✓	✓			4
48	Fairview Elementary	Dis	Adams County School Distr 50	✓	✓	✓			4

(continued)

Table A-1. (Continued)

Ref #	School Name	Type	Model or District	Att-bsd S Prog	Pers Lrng	Coll PBL	Crit-ref Assmt	Multiyear/ -age	Rating (1-5)
49	Flynn Elementary	Dis	Adams County School Distr 50	✓	✓	✓	✓		4
50	Harris Park Elementary	Dis	Adams County School Distr 50	✓	✓	✓	✓		4
51	Hidden Lake High School	Dis	Adams County School Distr 50	✓	✓	✓	✓		4
52	Hodgkins Elementary	Dis	Adams County School Distr 50	✓	✓	✓	✓		4
53	Mesa Elementary	Dis	Adams County School Distr 50	✓	✓	✓	✓		4
54	Metz Elementary	Dis	Adams County School Distr 50	✓	✓	✓	✓		4
55	Ranum Middle School	Dis	Adams County School Distr 50	✓	✓	✓	✓		4
56	Scott Carpenter Middle School	Dis	Adams County School Distr 50	✓	✓	✓	✓		4
57	Shaw Heights Middle School	Dis	Adams County School Distr 50	✓	✓	✓	✓		4
58	Sherrelwood Elementary	Dis	Adams County School Distr 50	✓	✓	✓	✓		4
59	Skyline Vista Elementary	Dis	Adams County School Distr 50	✓	✓	✓	✓		4
60	Sunset Ridge Elementary	Dis	Adams County School Distr 50	✓	✓	✓	✓		4

#	Name	Type	District						
61	Tennyson Knolls Elementary	Dis	Adams County School Distr 50		v	v	v		4
62	Westminster Elementary	Dis	Adams County School Distr 50		v	v	v		4
63	Westminster High School	Dis	Adams County School Distr 50		v	v	v		4
64	Carpe Diem Collegiate High School	Mod	Carpe Diem schools		v	v	v		4
65	Carpe Diem Collegiate High School dba Carpe Diem e-Learning Community	Mod	Carpe Diem schools		v	v	v		4
66	Aniak Jr. Sr. High School	Dis	Kuspuk School District		v	v	v	v	4
67	Auntie Mary Nicoli Elementary School	Dis	Kuspuk School District		v	v	v	v	4
68	Crow Village Sam School	Dis	Kuspuk School District		v	v	v	v	4
69	George Morgan Sr. High School	Dis	Kuspuk School District		v	v	v	v	4
70	Gusty Michael School	Dis	Kuspuk School District		v	v		v	4
71	Jack Egnaty Sr. School	Dis	Kuspuk School District		v	v		v	4
72	Johnnie John Sr. School	Dis	Kuspuk School District		v	v	v	v	4
73	Joseph & Olinga Gregory Elem Sch	Dis	Kuspuk School District		v	v	v	v	4
74	Zackar Levi Elementary School	Dis	Kuspuk School District		v	v	v	v	4
75	Chignik Bay School	Dis	Lake and Peninsula Schl Distr.	v	v	v		v	4
76	Chignik Lagoon School	Dis	Lake and Peninsula Schl Distr.	v	v			v	4
77	Chignik Lake School	Dis	Lake and Peninsula Schl Distr.	v	v			v	4
78	Egegik School	Dis	Lake and Peninsula Schl Distr.	v	v			v	4
79	Igiugig School	Dis	Lake and Peninsula Schl Distr.	v	v			v	4
80	Kokhanok School	Dis	Lake and Peninsula Schl Distr.	v	v			v	4

(continued)

Table A.1. *(Continued)*

Ref #	School Name	Type	Model or District	Att-bsd S Prog	Pers Lrng	Coll PBL	Crit-ref Assmt	Multiyear/ -age	Rating (1-5)
81	Levelock School	Dis	Lake and Peninsula Schl Distr.	v	v		v	v	4
82	Meshik School	Dis	Lake and Peninsula Schl Distr.	v	v		v	v	4
83	Newhalen School	Dis	Lake and Peninsula Schl Distr.	v	v		v	v	4
84	Nondalton School	Dis	Lake and Peninsula Schl Distr.	v	v		v	v	4
85	Perryville School	Dis	Lake and Peninsula Schl Distr.	v	v		v	v	4
86	Pilot Point School	Dis	Lake and Peninsula Schl Distr.	v	v		v	v	4
87	Tanalian School	Dis	Lake and Peninsula Schl Distr.	v	v		v	v	4
88	Lewis S. Libby School	Dis	Milford School District	v	v	v	v		4
89	Burchard A. Dunn School	Dis	MSAD 15 Gray New Gloucester	v	v	v	v		4
90	Gray-New Gloucester High School	Dis	MSAD 15 Gray New Gloucester	v	v	v	v		4
91	Gray-New Gloucester Middle School	Dis	MSAD 15 Gray New Gloucester	v	v	v	v		4
92	James W. Russell School	Dis	MSAD 15 Gray New Gloucester	v	v	v	v		4
93	Memorial School	Dis	MSAD 15 Gray New Gloucester	v	v	v	v		4
94	Manchester School of Technology	Ind	N/A	v	v	v	v		4
95	I.S. 228 David A. Boody Intermed Sch	Ind	N/A	v	v	v	v		4

#	School	Type	Network						Rating
96	I.S. 339 Tech Tigers	Ind	N/A	✓	✓	✓	✓		4
97	M.S.131 Dr. Sun Yat Sen Midl. Sch.	Ind	N/A	✓	✓	✓	✓		4
98	Nova High School	Ind	N/A	✓	✓	✓	✓	✓	4
99	The New School	Ind	N/A	✓	✓	✓	✓	✓	4
100	Pleasant View Elementary School	Ind	N/A	✓	✓	✓	✓		4
101	Ballard Brady Middle School	Dis	Next Generation Learning	✓	✓	✓	✓		4
102	Orange High School	Dis	Next Generation Learning	✓	✓	✓	✓		4
103	Moreland Hills Elementary School	Dis	Next Generation Learning	✓	✓	✓	✓		4
104	Kettle Moraine Global Charter Sch	Dis	Next Generation Learning	✓	✓	✓	✓	✓	4
105	Alakanuk School	Mod	Re-Inventing Schls. Coalition	✓	✓		✓	✓	4
106	Emmonak Public School	Mod	Re-Inventing Schls. Coalition	✓	✓	✓	✓	✓	4
107	Hooper Bay School	Mod	Re-Inventing Schls. Coalition	✓	✓	✓	✓	✓	4
108	Ignatius Beans Memorial School	Mod	Re-Inventing Schls. Coalition	✓	✓	✓	✓	✓	4
109	Kotlik School	Mod	Re-Inventing Schls. Coalition	✓	✓	✓	✓	✓	4
110	Marshall School	Mod	Re-Inventing Schls. Coalition	✓	✓	✓	✓	✓	4
111	Pilot Station	Mod	Re-Inventing Schls. Coalition	✓	✓	✓	✓	✓	4
112	Pitka's Point School	Mod	Re-Inventing Schls. Coalition	✓	✓		✓	✓	4

(continued)

Table A.1. *(Continued)*

Ref #	School Name	Type	Model or District	Att-bsd S Prog	Pers Lrng	Coll PBL	Crit-ref Assmt	Multiyr/age	Rating (1-5)
113	Russian Mission School	Mod	Re-Inventing Schls. Coalition	✓		✓	✓	✓	4
114	Scammon Bay School	Mod	Re-Inventing Schls. Coalition	✓		✓	✓	✓	4
115	Sheldon Point School	Mod	Re-Inventing Schls. Coalition	✓		✓	✓	✓	4
116	Barack Obama Charter School	Ind	Re-Inventing Schls. Coalition	✓	✓		✓	✓	4
117	Ingenium Charter School	Ind	Re-Inventing Schls. Coalition	✓	✓		✓	✓	4
118	Atwood Elementary School	Dis	RSU 18 Messalonskee	✓	✓	✓	✓		4
119	Belgrade Central Elementary School	Dis	RSU 18 Messalonskee	✓	✓	✓	✓		4
120	China Middle School	Dis	RSU 18 Messalonskee	✓	✓	✓	✓		4
121	China Primary School	Dis	RSU 18 Messalonskee	✓	✓	✓	✓		4
122	James H. Bean Elementary School	Dis	RSU 18 Messalonskee	✓	✓	✓	✓		4
123	Messalonskee High School	Dis	RSU 18 Messalonskee	✓	✓	✓	✓		4
124	Messalonskee Middle School	Dis	RSU 18 Messalonskee	✓	✓	✓	✓		4
125	Williams Elementary School	Dis	RSU 18 Messalonskee	✓	✓	✓	✓		4
126	Dresden Elementary School	Dis	RSU 2 Hallowell	✓	✓	✓	✓		4
127	Hall-Dale Elementary School	Dis	RSU 2 Hallowell	✓	✓	✓	✓		4
128	Hall-Dale High School	Dis	RSU 2 Hallowell	✓	✓	✓	✓		4
129	Hall-Dale Middle School	Dis	RSU 2 Hallowell	✓	✓	✓	✓		4
130	Henry L. Cottrell Elementary School	Dis	RSU 2 Hallowell	✓	✓	✓	✓		4
131	Marcia Buker Elementary School	Dis	RSU 2 Hallowell	✓	✓	✓	✓		4
132	Monmouth Academy	Dis	RSU 2 Hallowell	✓	✓	✓	✓		4

133	Monmouth Middle School	Dis	RSU 2 Hallowell	✓	✓	✓	4
134	Richmond High School	Dis	RSU 2 Hallowell	✓	✓	✓	4
135	Richmond Middle School	Dis	RSU 2 Hallowell	✓	✓	✓	4
136	Alfread Elementary School	Dis	RSU 57 Massebesic	✓	✓	✓	4
137	Line Elementary School	Dis	RSU 57 Massebesic	✓	✓	✓	4
138	Lyman Elementary School	Dis	RSU 57 Massebesic	✓	✓	✓	4
139	Massabesic High School	Dis	RSU 57 Massebesic	✓	✓	✓	4
140	Messabesic Middle School	Dis	RSU 57 Massebesic	✓	✓	✓	4
141	Shapleigh Memorial School	Dis	RSU 57 Massebesic	✓	✓	✓	4
142	Waterboro Elementary School	Dis	RSU 57 Massebesic	✓	✓	✓	4
143	Forest Hills Consolidated School	Dis	RSU 82 Jackman	✓	✓	✓	4
144	George Washington Middle School	Ind	West Virginia District of Educ.	✓	✓	✓	4
145	Monroe County Technical Center	Ind	West Virginia District of Educ.	✓	✓	✓	4

Appendix B

So What If Paradigm Change Takes a Long Time?

It is worth pausing to think what is likely to happen in the absence of paradigm change in education. For starters, Lesley Morrow, the past president of the International Reading Association, stated that some states determine how many prison cells to build based on reading scores. How sad—for our culture and our economy—because it costs far more per year to incarcerate a person than to educate them, and the "opportunity cost" of a person being locked away instead of contributing to the workforce and paying taxes costs communities dearly, too, not to mention the value of lives murdered and goods stolen or destroyed.

There's also the cost of a workforce that cannot compete in a global economy. Many knowledge-work jobs can be performed anywhere in the world. If U.S. workers are unable to obtain and hold high-paying, high-value jobs, this nation will experience a general lowering of the standard of living. Add to that the cost to society of not sufficiently developing the talents of our most creative and capable students.

Furthermore, there is the human cost of many individuals being far from reaching their potential and thereby enduring a diminished quality of life. The Information Age education paradigm is concerned with the complete, well-rounded development of each child, which includes his nutrition, health, and quality of life as well as his character development and values. There is evidence that such a focus on character development and values in smaller, caring learning environments has a significant impact on substance abuse, violence, and incarceration. What are the costs of continuing with these rates in the United States among the highest in the world?

The costs associated with continued investment and participation in an educational system outdated and no longer meeting the needs of our students and citizens are enormous. The United States is at a crossroads. Can we transform education to retain our position as world leader, or will we fail to correct the course we're on to decay into the control of other, more motivated potential world leaders?

Appendix C
Tools for Paradigm Change

Here is a brief introduction to some conceptual tools from systems thinking that you might find helpful:

- Peter Senge's iceberg
- Peter Senge's ladder of inference
- Peter Senge's eleven laws of systems
- Bela Banathy's three views of systems
- Russell Ackoff's four orientations to change
- Charles Reigeluth's fractals from chaos theory
- Frank Duffy's three paths to transformation

SENGE'S ICEBERG

The iceberg represents one kind of systems thinking. Peter Senge argues that much of what needs to be changed in a system is beneath the surface, out of sight. What you can see are events that occur throughout the system. More difficult to see, just beneath the surface, are recurring patterns that those events form. For example, many teachers have noticed the pattern of fads in education whereby a hot new initiative is mandated by the central office, teachers who don't think much of it don't try very hard to implement it, the initiative doesn't work out as well as anticipated, and the initiative is abandoned. It is not long before a new fad comes along and goes through the same pattern.

Even further beneath the surface and thus more difficult to see are the system structures that produce those patterns of events. Most difficult to see (and to change) are the mental models of people in the system that allow those structures to continue. Therefore, mental models represent the true core of problems in a system and are keys to transforming the system.

Senge uses the image of an iceberg to characterize this important aspect of systems thinking:

- *Events* are the part of the iceberg above the water. They are identified by asking, "What just happened?"
- *Patterns* are just out of sight, below the surface of the water. They are identified by asking, "What's been happening? Have we been here or someplace similar before?"
- *System structures* are the next deeper part of the iceberg. They are identified by asking, "What are the forces at play contributing to those patterns?"
- *Mental models* are the deepest part of the iceberg. They are identified by asking, "What about our thinking allows this situation to persist?" (Senge, 2000, p. 127).

The implication of this iceberg is that paradigm change requires a change in mental models to bring about changes in system structures, that in turn will enable changes in patterns of events to occur.

SENGE'S LADDER OF INFERENCE

The ladder of inference is a visual representation of a person's faulty thinking. Most people think their beliefs are the truth, that the truth is obvious, that their beliefs are based on real data, and that the selected data are the real data. Based on belief, people climb a "ladder of inference" by creating a reality that may or may not be real.

The rungs of the ladder are as follows:

- I take: actions (based on my beliefs)
- I adopt: beliefs (about the world)
- I draw: conclusions
- I make: assumptions (based on the meanings I added)
- I add: meanings (cultural and personal)
- I select: "data" (from what I observe)

On the ground are observable "data" and experiences (as a video recording might capture it). (Senge, 2000, p. 102).

Someone says something or looks a certain way or uses a gesture and another person starts the assent by assuming that what he thinks is happening is, in fact, happening. People make assumptions based on their mental filters.

To aid in communication, the ladder of inference can be avoided by making the thinking process visible and shared. Ask:

- What are the observable data?
- Do we all agree on what the data are?
- Can you walk me through your reasoning?
- How did we get from that data to these abstract assumptions?

Only by confronting their assumptions and misperceived beliefs by checking them out with others can a person understand what is really being communicated. This is especially important for helping participants to evolve their mental models during a paradigm change process.

SENGE'S ELEVEN LAWS OF SYSTEMS

Another kind of systems thinking is represented by Senge's eleven laws:

1. *Today's problems come from yesterday's solutions.* People tend to solve problems without understanding the unintended consequences of their solutions. These create new problems that may be even more difficult to solve.
2. *The harder you push, the harder the system pushes back.* Every action creates a reaction. Well-intentioned interventions "call forth responses from the system that offset the benefits of the intervention."[1]
3. *Behavior grows better before it grows worse.* Compared to long-term solutions, it is easier to find short-term solutions that give temporary improvement but don't eliminate the fundamental problems. In the long run, the problems become worse.
4. *The easy way out leads back in.* There are seldom simple solutions in complex systems. If the solution was easy, the problem would have been solved already.
5. *The cure can be worse than the disease.* Easy solutions can create more problems than they solve.
6. *Faster is slower.* As in the race between the rabbit and tortoise, it is tempting to run at full speed. However, rushing to accomplish things can result in inadequate development of mental models that are crucial for success.

7. *Cause and effect are not always closely related in time and space.* This makes it difficult to understand all the effects of actions one plans to take, and equally difficult to understand all the factors that have contributed to today's problems.

8. *Small changes can produce big results, but the areas of highest leverage are often the least obvious.* Making the right changes can make transformation faster and more successful, but it is often difficult to tell what those high-leverage changes will be.

9. *You can have your cake and eat it too—but not all at once.* Systems thinkers avoid thinking in terms of "either/or" choices. Rather, "both/and" thinking often leads to important breakthroughs.

10. *Dividing an elephant in half does not produce two small elephants.* Often, people fail to see the system as a whole. A focus on parts can produce problems like suboptimal decisions, repeated tasks, lost time and energy, and even losing followers.

11. *There is no blame.* Although people tend to blame each other or blame forces outside the system, the real enemy is the system itself. The solution lies within the system.

BANATHY'S THREE VIEWS OF SYSTEMS

Banathy advocates looking at systems through these three lenses or views:

The *bird's-eye view* shows the external relationships between a system and other systems (both superordinate and coordinate), including input-output relationships and complex causal dynamics. Some systems are tightly controlled by their superordinate systems (suprasystems); others are loosely controlled. The tighter the control that one system has over another system, the more important it is for the controlled system to bring about changes in the suprasystem (or loosen its control) to make a paradigm change.

The *still-picture view* shows the internal relationships among the subsystems that make up a system. It offers a "snapshot in time" of the system that includes seeing its purpose and goals, how all its subsystems are structured (what relationships exist among them), what functions they serve, who the key players are in each subsystem, what roles each person plays, individual spheres of influence, policies and other rules influencing the behavior of subsystems, and so forth. The *coherence* of subsystems is an indicator of how compatible they are with each other and how well they support each other and the larger system.

The *motion-picture view* shows two kinds of motion that apply to systems: processes and cause-effect relationships. Systems receive inputs and perform processes to produce outputs. One can map the processes to describe them from beginning to end, and paradigm change entails reengineering the processes to make them more effective and efficient. Causal dynamics within a system can make or break any effort to change the system. Understanding those causal effects and how different parts of the process affect each other and the outcomes is critical.

ACKOFF'S FOUR ORIENTATIONS TO CHANGE

Russell Ackoff introduced four ways that people perceive and respond to change (see table C.1):

- reactive style
- inactive style
- preactive style
- interactive style

Ackoff also described the implications of each style for one's general attitude toward change, perception of the role of science and technology, organizational mode and culture, approach to planning and problem solving, and attractiveness of the orientation.

REIGELUTH'S FRACTALS FROM CHAOS THEORY

A new science can help us transform complex organizations such as educational systems. It is called the *science of complexity*, which is a pretty intimidating name, we know. And the science of complexity includes *chaos theory*, but don't let that scare you away. A very simple yet powerful notion in chaos theory can help us figure out how to really improve education for children. It's a notion called *fractals*.

Fractals are simply patterns that recur on all levels of a system. Notice that the pattern you see in figure C.1—when you look at the picture on a broad, global level—is repeated when you look at one major part of the picture, and it repeats again when you look at a part of a part.

But what does this have to do with educational systems? In educational systems, fractals are *core ideas* and values or beliefs that characterize the

Table C.1. Ackoff's Four Orientations to Change

	Reactive Style	Inactive Style	Preactive Style	Interactive Style
General attitude	Although people are not satisfied with the present, they don't focus on where we want to go.	People tend to believe that as long as things are good enough, no change is needed.	People anticipate change, prepare for it when it arrives, and exploit its opportunities.	People believe that the future depends more "on what we do between now and then than it does on what has happened until now."
Perception of the role of science and technology	People regard technology and science as the main cause of bad consequences of change.	People rely on present practices rather than referring to science as a guide and are hesitant to adopt new technology.	People use science-based methods in order to foresee the future and promote technology as a panacea.	People believe that the value of technology is manifested in the way we make purposeful use of it as a tool.
Organizational mode and culture	People rely on hierarchical, bureaucratic, and top-down old organizational forms.	The operational mode is bureaucratic, and conformity is valued more than creativity.	People want to become number one by pursuing novelty and growth rather than conformity.	People integrate their systems, operating at the various levels of the systems complex, through continuous and purposeful interaction.
Approach to planning and working with problems	People suggest only the piecemeal option to solve problems and believe they can achieve what they want.	Planning focuses on extrapolation from the present, and problems are treated in a piecemeal way.	Planning relies on predictions for preparing for the future, and people search for new techniques in order to be on the cutting edge of technology.	People engage in two major operations: designing the desired future and planning for implementing it.
Attractiveness	Three main attractions: history from which we can derive guidance, continuity, and tradition	People believe that problems fade away if left alone, and those who act cautiously seldom make mistakes.	Close association with modern science and technology accounts for much of its great appeal as well as its prestige.	People feel empowered to create their own future.

Figure C.1.   A Fractal Showing Patterns That Recur on Different Levels

system on all of its levels, which include the district, school, and classroom levels. Here are some examples:

Top-down Control

One example of a fractal in our current educational system is top-down control. On the district level, the superintendent controls the central-office administrators and the school principals. On the school level, the principals control their teachers. And on the classroom level, the teachers control their students. The same pattern (top-down control) is repeated on all levels of the system.

Uniformity

Another fractal example is uniformity or standardization. On the district level, all elementary schools are typically supposed to be the same in key features such as policies, curriculum, methods, and assessments. On the school level, all teachers at the same grade level are supposed to teach the same content at the same time with the same textbooks. On the classroom level, all students in a classroom are typically supposed to learn the same thing at the same time in the same way. Again, the same pattern (uniformity) is repeated on all levels of the system.

Top-down control and uniformity are but two of many fractals that characterize our factory model of schools. While we are beginning to see changes in some of these patterns, few would argue that they are atypical in the still-at-play Industrial Age education systems.

We cannot change the paradigm without changing the fractals that make up the deep structure of our educational systems.

Here are new fractals needed for the Information Age education paradigm:

Empowerment

Top-down control needs to be replaced by empowerment. Empowerment means having the *freedom* to make decisions and receiving *support* for making and acting on those decisions.

On the district level, this means that the school board and superintendent empower each school principal to experiment with and adopt new approaches to better meet student needs and to make other important decisions such as hiring and budgeting. At the school level, the principal empowers each teacher to experiment with and adopt new instructional approaches and resources to better meet students' needs and to participate in school policy making and decision making. On the classroom level, the teacher empowers each student to make decisions about how to best meet her information needs.

Customization

On the district level, a customization fractal means that each school has the freedom to be different from other schools. On the school level, each teacher is encouraged to teach differently (in terms of content and methods) from other teachers. And on the classroom level, students pursue diverse subjects of study and methods for learning.

Shared Decision Making

A collaboration fractal on the district level means that the school board and superintendent involve each school and its stakeholders in policymaking and decision-making. On the school level, the principal includes parents, teachers, and staff in decisions about operations and policies. And on the classroom level, the teacher encourages students and parents to participate in decisions and activities that promote the child's development.

These fractals are characteristics listed in table 1-1. They reflect a fundamental transformation from the Industrial Age to the Information Age. But they are more than characteristics of an organization; they require changes in how people think about education. And when those changes in thinking take place in a large enough percentage of stakeholders to become cultural norms, they can spur a legitimate transformation of the education system, and very little planning needs to be done for the transformation to take place.

DUFFY'S THREE PATHS FOR PARADIGM CHANGE

Frank Duffy, an expert in paradigm change in education, has identified three paths that are required for paradigm change: the system's work processes, the system's social infrastructure, and the system's relationship with its systemic environment.

Work Processes

The *primary work processes* are teaching and learning, and they must be transformed from teacher-centered to learner-centered. Many other *supporting work processes* are performed in a school system, including administrative processes such as hiring, firing, payroll, accounting, and purchasing; food service; transportation; cleaning and maintenance; library services; professional development; technology support; and scheduling. And many of these supporting work processes must be redesigned to be compatible with the redesigned primary work processes. Therefore, it is helpful to understand ways in which a particular supporting work process impacts the core work process, other supporting work processes, and individuals in the system.

Social Infrastructure

This includes organization culture, communication practices, job descriptions, reward systems, and more. These must be transformed from those appropriate for a command-and-control organization to those for a participatory organization.

Relationships with the Systemic Environment

Relationships must be transformed from ones whereby schools *isolate* themselves from their communities and only *react* to pressures from their communities to ones that entail *collaborating* with and *proactively* dealing with their communities about issues related to education.

These three paths must be traveled simultaneously, given the interdependencies among them.

NOTE

1. P. M. Senge, *The Fifth Discipline: The Art and Practice of the Learning Organization* (New York: Doubleday, 1990).

RELATED READINGS

Ackoff, R. L. *Creating the Corporate Future.* New York: Wiley, 1981.

Banathy, B. H. *Systems Design of Education: A Journey to Create the Future.* Englewood Cliffs, N.J.: Educational Technology Publications, 1991.

———. *A Systems View of Education: Concepts and Principles for Effective Practice.* Englewood Cliffs, NJ: Educational Technology Publications, 1992.

———. *Designing Social Systems in a Changing World.* New York: Plenum Press, 1996.

Duffy, F. M. *Step-Up-to-Excellence: An Innovative Approach to Managing and Rewarding Performance in School Systems.* Lanham, MD: Scarecrow Education, 2002.

Duffy, F. M., and C. M. Reigeluth. "The School System Transformation (SST) Protocol." *Educational Technology* 48, no. 4 (2008): 41–49.

Hammer, M., and J. Champy. *Reengineering the Corporation: A Manifesto for Business Revolution.* New York: HarperBusiness, 2001.

Senge, P. M. *The Fifth Discipline: The Art and Practice of the Learning Organization.* New York: Doubleday, 1990.

———. *Schools That Learn: A Fifth Discipline Fieldbook for Educators, Parents, and Everyone Who Cares about Education.* New York: Doubleday, 2000.

Index

About the Authors

Charles M. Reigeluth felt frustration with his own schooling, so he decided when he was sixteen years old to devote his career to help make education a lot more motivating, effective, and efficient. He taught high school for three years, was a professor at Indiana University doing field research for twenty-five years, and helped a small school district in Indianapolis to engage in a reinvention process for twelve years.

Jennifer R. Karnopp has a master's degree in special education and has been an advocate for child-centered education for the past twenty years, working in both traditional schools and nontraditional education settings. Most recently, she is a founder and current Head of School at the Robert Frost Charter School in North Conway, New Hampshire.